D0180737

Voyage

THE COAST OF UTOPIA PART I

Tom Stoppard's other work includes *Enter a Free Man*, *Rosencrantz and Guildenstern Are Dead*, *The Real Inspector Hound*, *Jumpers*, *Travesties*, *Night and Day*, *Every Good Boy Deserves Favour* (with Andre Previn), *After Magritte*, *Dirty Linen*, *The Real Thing*, *Hapgood*, *Arcadia*, *Indian Ink* and *The Invention of Love*. His radio plays include: *If You're Glad, I'll Be Frank*, *Albert's Bridge*, *Where Are They Now?*, *Artist Descending a Staircase*, *The Dog It Was That Died* and *in the Native State*. His work for television includes *Professional Foul* and *Squaring the Circle*. His film credits include *Empire of the Sun*, *Rosencrantz and Guildenstern Are Dead*, which he also directed, *Shakespeare in Love* (with Marc Norman) and *Enigma*.

HELEN HALL LIBRARY
City of League City
100 West Walker
League City, Texas 77573-3899

DISCARD

JAN   2004

TOM STOPPARD

Voyage

THE COAST OF UTOPIA
PART I

HELEN HALL LIBRARY
City of League City
100 West Walker
League City, Texas 77573-3899

DISCARD

Grove Press
New York

Copyright © 2002 by Tom Stoppard

All rights reserved. No part of this book may be reproduced in any form or by any electronic or mechanical means, including information storage and retrieval systems, without permission in writing from the publisher, except by a reviewer, who may quote brief passages in a review. Any members of educational institutions wishing to photocopy part or all of the work for classroom use, or publishers who would like to obtain permission to include the work in an anthology, should send their inquiries to Grove/Atlantic, Inc., 841 Broadway, New York, NY 10003.

CAUTION: Professionals and amateurs are hereby warned that *Voyage: The Coast of Utopia Part I* is subject to a royalty. It is fully protected under the copyright laws of the United States, Canada, United Kingdom, and all British Commonwealth countries, and all countries covered by the International Copyright Union, the Pan-American Copyright Convention, and the Universal Copyright Convention. All rights, including professional, amateur, motion picture, recitation, public reading, radio broadcasting, television, video or sound taping, all other forms of mechanical or electronic reproduction, such as information storage and retrieval systems and photocopying, and rights of translation into foreign languages, are strictly reserved.

First-class professional, stock, and amateur applications for permission to perform it, and those other rights stated above, must be made in advance to Peters, Fraser & Dunlop, Drury House, 34–43 Russell Street, London, WC2B 5HA, England, ATTN: Kenneth Ewing, and must pay the requisite fee, whether the play is presented for charity or gain and whether or not admission is charged.

First published in hardback and paperback in 2002 by Faber and Faber Limited, London, England

Printed in the United States of America

FIRST AMERICAN EDITION

Library of Congress Cataloging-in-Publication Data

Stoppard, Tom.
  Voyage / Tom Stoppard.
    p. cm. — (The Coast of Utopia ; pt. 1)
  ISBN 0-8021-4004-1 (pbk)
  ISBN 0-8021-1760-0 (hc)
  ISBN 0-8021-4003-3 (boxed set)
  1. Bakunin, Mikhail Aleksandrovich, 1814–1876—Drama. 2. Herzen,
Aleksandr, 1812–1870—Drama. 3. Russians—Germany—Drama.
4. Moscow (Russia)—Drama. 5. Revolutionaries—Drama. 6. Anarchists—Drama.
7. Germany—Drama. I. Title.
  PR6069.T6V695 2003
  822'.914—dc21

                                                                    2003042181

Grove Press
841 Broadway
New York, NY 10003

03 04 05 06 07   10 9 8 7 6 5 4 3 2 1

I am gratefully indebted to Trevor Nunn
for encouraging me towards some additions
and subtractions while *The Coast of Utopia*
was in rehearsal

ACKNOWLEDGMENTS

I would like to thank, first, Aileen Kelly, who has written extensively about Alexander Herzen and Mikhail Bakunin. I am indebted to her for her kindness as well as her scholarship. Moreover, Dr Kelly is, with Henry Hardy, who also has my gratitude for our exchanges, the coeditor of the book which was my entry to the world of *The Coast of Utopia*, namely *Russian Thinkers*, a selection of essays by Isaiah Berlin. Berlin is one of two authors without whom I could not have written these plays, the other being E. H. Carr, whose *The Romantic Exiles* is in print again after nearly seventy years, and whose biography of Bakunin deserves to be. I received valuable help from Helen Rappaport on Russian matters in general. I am particularly indebted to her for Russian translation, including lines of dialogue. Krista Jussenhoven kindly made up for my deficiency in German, Rose Cobbe corrected my French, and Sonja Nerdrum supplied me with the lines in Italian. My thanks to all of them, and to the Royal National Institute for the Deaf for access to its library.

Voyage was first performed in the Olivier Auditorium of the National Theatre, London, as the first part of *The Coast of Utopia* trilogy, on June 27, 2002. The cast was as follows:

ALEXANDER BAKUNIN John Carlisle

VARVARA Felicity Dean

LIUBOV Eve Best

VARENKA Charlotte Emmerson

TATIANA Lucy Whybrow

ALEXANDRA Anna Maxwell Martin

MISS CHAMBERLAIN Jennifer Scott Malden

BARON RENNE Jack James

SEMYON John Nolan

MICHAEL BAKUNIN Douglas Henshall

NICHOLAS STANKEVICH Raymond Coulthard

MASHA Janet Spencer-Turner

VISSARION BELINSKY Will Keen

IVAN TURGENEV Guy Henry

ALEXANDER HERZEN Stephen Dillane

MRS BEYER Janine Duvitski

NICHOLAS SAZONOV Jonathan Slinger

NICHOLAS OGAREV Simon Day

NICHOLAS KETSCHER Paul Ritter

NICHOLAS POLEVOY Nick Sampson

NATALIE BEYER Rachel Ferjani

PETER CHAADAEV Iain Mitchell

STEPAN SHEVYREV Sam Troughton

DYAKOV David Verrey

KATYA Jasmine Hyde

PUSHKIN Jack James

A GINGER CAT Richard Hollis

Other parts played by Thomas Arnold, Martin Chamberlain, Sarah Manton, Kemal Sylvester

Director Trevor Nunn
Set, Costume and Video Designer William Dudley
Lighting Designer David Hersey
Associate Director Stephen Rayne
Music Steven Edis
Movement Director David Bolger
Sound Designer Paul Groothuis
Company Voice Work Patsy Rodenburg

CHARACTERS

ALEXANDER BAKUNIN

VARVARA, *his wife*

LIUBOV
VARENKA
TATIANA
ALEXANDRA
} *their daughters*

MISS CHAMBERLAIN, *an English governess*

BARON RENNE, *a cavalry officer*

SEMYON, *senior household servant*

MASHA, *the maid*

NICHOLAS STANKEVICH, *a young philosopher*

MICHAEL BAKUNIN, *the Bakunins' son*

VISSARION BELINSKY, *a literary critic*

IVAN TURGENEV, *a would-be writer*

ALEXANDER HERZEN, *a would-be revolutionary*

NICHOLAS SAZONOV
NICHOLAS OGAREV
NICHOLAS KETSCHER
} *Herzen's 'circle'*

NICHOLAS POLEVOY, *editor of the* Telegraph

MRS BEYER

NATALIE BEYER, *Mrs Beyer's daughter*

PETER CHAADAEV, *a philosopher*

THE COAST OF UTOPIA

STEPAN SHEVYREV, *editor of the* Moscow Observer

KATYA, *Belinsky's mistress*

ALEXANDER PUSHKIN, *the poet*

DYAKOV, *a cavalry officer*

A GINGER CAT

SERVANT, PARTY GUESTS, MUSICIANS, ETC.

Voyage

ACT ONE

Summer 1833

Premukhino, the Bakunin estate, a hundred and fifty miles north-west of Moscow.

Interior, verandah, garden. There are places to sit in the garden, and a hammock. One setting is intended to serve for Act One.

Family supper is coming to an end. At the table—ALEXANDER BAKUNIN (sixty-five) and his wife, VARVARA (forty-two); their daughters, LIUBOV (twenty-two), VARENKA (twenty-one), TATIANA (eighteen) and ALEXANDRA (seventeen); MISS CHAMBERLAIN, a young English governess; and BARON RENNE (thirty-six), a cavalry officer in uniform. Household servants (serfs), notably SEMYON, who is senior, attend the table as may be. 'English' dialogue is spoken with a Russian accent, except in the case of Miss Chamberlain. The tempo is lively. Alexander Bakunin's rule is benign despotism, but the family atmosphere is prevailingly democratic.

ALEXANDER Speaking of which—Liubov, say something in English for the Baron.

LIUBOV What do you want me to say, Papa?

ALEXANDER All my daughters have been educated in five languages—call me a liberal if you like, I read Rousseau as a young man, I was there at the storming of the Bastille, not storming it personally but I remember *my* feelings were decidedly mixed, that's how liberal I was when I was nineteen. But education for women, yes indeed!—not just

1

piano lessons and Russian grammar *pour les filles* Bakunin, though mind you, they write better Russian than I do— what a shame there's nothing worth reading (*over his daughters' protests*), apart from . . .

DAUGHTERS   Pushkin!

ALEXANDER   . . . Pushkin. But I tell you, Baron, in choosing my eldest daughter you have chosen the cleverest—

VARVARA   I prefer Kozlov.

ALEXANDER   —brains before beauty, I wish I'd done the same—

DAUGHTERS   Oh shame!—Shame on you, Papa—I hereby protest on behalf of my beautiful sister—Don't you listen, Liubov—

VARVARA   Quiet when your father is speaking—

MISS CHAMBERLAIN   What did your father say?

LIUBOV   I take it as a compliment, Papa.

VARVARA   So do I.

TATIANA   The Baron doesn't think so, do you?

RENNE   No! No . . . Liubov is as beautiful as your wife is intelligent.

ALEXANDER   That's what I said. What a diplomat! Come on, Liubov, my darling, we're waiting.

LIUBOV   I'm sure the Baron doesn't want . . .

ALEXANDRA   I can, Papa! (*She pops up, standing rigid. In 'English'*) 'How do you do, Baron Renne! I say! charming weather, you do not think!'

She sits just as suddenly, and Tatiana follows suit.

TATIANA (*in 'English'*) 'The quality of mercy is not strained, it dropping like the gentle dew from heaven!'

Tatiana sits. Alexander continues imperturbably.

ALEXANDER I myself was educated in Italy. My doctorate in philosophy is from the University of Padua.

MISS CHAMBERLAIN Jolly good effort, Tatiana.

RENNE Really? Philosophy?

VARVARA What did she say?

ALEXANDER My dissertation was on worms.

TATIANA Shakespeare, *Maman*.

RENNE Worms the philosopher?

ALEXANDER No, just worms.

VARVARA I mean Miss Chamberlain, *qu'est-ce qu'ele a dit?* [What did she say?]

RENNE Ah, the philosophy of *worms*.

VARENKA *Elle l'a félicitée, Maman, c'est tout.* [Good effort, Maman, that's all.]

ALEXANDER Not at all. Worms have no philosophy, as far as is known.

VARVARA How can you teach them anything if you can't talk to them?

ALEXANDER Exactly.

MISS CHAMBERLAIN I'm so sorry, what did your mother say?

ALEXANDRA (*in 'English'*) 'No lessons tomorrow, she said, holiday.'

MISS CHAMBERLAIN I think not, see me afterwards.

ALEXANDER That's enough English for now. Anyway, a wife who knows English is not the first consideration for an officer in the Cavalry, otherwise you'd be better off with the governess—No, I only have one serious objection to this marriage, my dear Baron—

DAUGHTERS Oh, no!—What's he going to say next?!—Don't you listen, Liubov!—Father, don't—!

VARVARA (*raps the table*) *Enough!*

ALEXANDER Thank you. What was I saying? Oh, well, it's gone.

RENNE Actually, I have to be going myself while there's still light in the sky, if you forgive me, it's a good ride back to camp—

VARVARA Yes, you must, it wouldn't do to break your neck before the happy day, or after, of course.

Noises of arrival and greeting are heard.

ALEXANDER What's going on?

RENNE A thousand thanks—(*for Liubov, gallantly*)—a thousand and one—

VARENKA Someone's come.

SEMYON (*entering*) It's Michael, sir, large as life! He's come home!

MICHAEL BAKUNIN *is nineteen, in uniform. His entry causes an excited and emotional reunion, as 'the table' breaks up.*

FAMILY   Michael!—Oh my, look at you!—Why didn't you let us know?—So grown up! Look at his uniform!—Let me kiss you!—You're not in trouble, are you? I prayed and prayed for you—How long are you staying?—

MICHAEL   No, I'm on leave—I came straight from summer exercises!—

ALEXANDER   It's my boy, he's an ensign in the Artillery.

RENNE   Of course—the famous Michael.

LIUBOV (*to Renne*)   Thank you for your visit, I'm sorry my family is . . .

RENNE   Oh no, you're all so . . . wonderfully unrussian . . .

MICHAEL   And congratulations are in order, I believe. Do I have the honour . . . ?

LIUBOV   Baron Renne—I present my brother Michael—

RENNE   You have been at the Artillery School in Peter?

ALEXANDRA   For five years!

ALEXANDER (*to Miss Chamberlain*)   Run and tell Semyon to bring champagne. 'Command Semyon to provision—'

MISS CHAMBERLAIN (*running out*)   Champagne, champagne, I understand—

TATIANA   Our English governess, do you think she's pretty?

MICHAEL   No, I think you're pretty.

RENNE (*tapping his glass*)   Ladies and gentlemen! (*addressing Michael*) The Cavalry drinks to the Artillery. But a family reunion is a sacred affair, and I was just saying good night—regimental duties, who understands better than you? So farewell! I embrace you, and am proud to call you brother!

Applause from the family. Michael and Renne shake hands and embrace.

ALEXANDER   Good! Come along, we'll give you a proper send-off. Semyon!—Pavel!—one of you—his horse—the Baron is leaving!—

A general exodus begins.

ALEXANDER *(cont.)* *(remembering)*   Ah, yes. That was it. I have only one serious doubt about this marriage—

LIUBOV *(tearfully)*   Father . . .

VARENKA *(to Liubov)*   It's a joke.

ALEXANDER   . . . and that is the difference in your ages.

RENNE   But I'm only thirty-six!

ALEXANDER   A good ten years too young for her! The husband should be at least twice the age of the wife.

VARVARA   But you're not.

ALEXANDER   Not *now*, of course. *(to Renne)* Beauty before brains.

ALEXANDRA   Are you coming, Michael?

TATIANA *(hanging back)*   Yes, he's coming.

MICHAEL *(to Liubov)*   Do you want to see him off without everybody . . . ?

LIUBOV *(hastily)*   No, no, let's all go.

ALEXANDER   Family on parade! . . . Handkerchiefs for waving and weeping—*(to Renne)* My wife was eighteen and I was forty-two. See my point?—just when the wife starts getting

a mind to kick over the traces, she realises she only has to
show a little patience . . .

Michael, Varenka and Tatiana are left alone.

MICHAEL   Well! *He* won't do! Liubov doesn't love him, that's
obvious.

VARENKA   We know *that*.

TATIANA   She won't go against Papa, and the Baron is a good
match, isn't he?

*Semyon enters with a tray of champagne glasses, and Miss
Chamberlain with a bottle. Voices outside: 'Tatiana! Michael! And
where's Varenka?'*

MICHAEL   Thank you, Semyon. Leave us be.

*Semyon leaves deferentially. Miss Chamberlain, unwisely, approaches
gushing.*

MISS CHAMBERLAIN   So you are Michael.

MICHAEL   'Go away, please.'

*Miss Chamberlain gasps. The girls are shocked and admiring. Miss
Chamberlain runs out. From outside 'Varenka!' is called. Varenka
runs out.*

MICHAEL (*cont.*)   I'm speaking of love and you are speaking of
matchmaking. Tata, Tata, don't you know? Dawn has
broken! In Germany the sun is already high in the sky! It's
only us in poor behind-the-times Russia who are the last to
learn about the great discovery of the age! The life of the
Spirit is the only real life: our everyday existence stands
between us and our transcendence to the Universal Idea
where we become one with the Absolute! Do you see?

TATIANA (*desperately*)   Tell it to me in German.

MICHAEL   This marriage cannot take place. We must save
  Liubov. To give oneself without love is a sin against the
  inner life. The outer world of material existence is mere
  illusion. I'll explain it all to Father.

Tatiana and Michael are being called from outside. She launches
herself at Michael to embrace him, and runs out.

MICHAEL (*cont.*)   God, I'm *starving!*

Michael pauses to stuff his mouth with food from the table, then
follows Tatiana.

SPRING 1835

Garden and verandah.

Varvara comes out onto the verandah.

VARVARA   Where are you all? The newlyweds are here!

Liubov appears in the garden.

LIUBOV   *Maman*, they've been married for months.

VARVARA   You wouldn't be so calm if you knew what I
  know!

She sees Tatiana and Alexandra and calls to them before hurrying
back inside.

VARVARA (*cont.*)   Come on!—Varenka's here with her
  husband.

Tatiana and Alexandra enter, making a beeline for Liubov and beside
themselves with outrage. Alexandra has a letter.

ALEXANDRA   Liubov! Michael's in love with guess who, Natalie Beyer!

TATIANA   No, he's not, she's in love with *him*. The nerve of the woman!

VARVARA (*reappearing crossly*)   Tatiana!

TATIANA   We're coming, Mother, what's all the fuss?

LIUBOV   Varenka's having a baby.

VARVARA (*panicked*)   Who told you?

LIUBOV   You did.

VARVARA   I did not, I did not! You don't know, do you hear, you don't know. (*She darts back inside.*)

TATIANA (*sobered*)   Poor Varenka!

ALEXANDRA   Aunties! What a day!

LIUBOV   What's happened?

ALEXANDRA   Michael's back from Moscow and he's brought this *stupid* letter from Natalie Beyer . . . listen, it's to you too, are you ready? 'My friends! I take up my pen as a duty to myself, to you, and to the Universal Idea. Michael has opened his heart to me. Ah, if only you knew the Michael I know! If only you understood him!'

TATIANA   Imbecile!

LIUBOV   But in Moscow she was all over Nicholas Stankevich.

TATIANA   It's because Nicholas Stankevich likes *you*. (*Liubov demurs.*) Yes, he does, he led Natalie up the garden; she told us. Go on, Alexandra!

ALEXANDRA 'With all the love you bear him, you can't see that Michael's virile and vigorous nature is being frustrated by your'—yes, my friends, *your*—listen to this—'limited progress in transcending the objective reality in which you see him only as your brother—'

LIUBOV What's he been complaining about?

TATIANA Not getting his own way in everything, I suppose.

LIUBOV None of her business. Anyway, he does.

ALEXANDRA There's lots more.

But Varenka comes from inside, her eyes brimming with emotion. Her pregnancy does not show.

VARENKA Oh, there you are! It's just us . . . Oh good.

ALEXANDRA Varenka!—look at this. From Natalie Beyer!

TATIANA She's after Michael!

LIUBOV Varenka . . . !

ALEXANDRA Can you believe the little minx?

Then they recall themselves to Varenka, suddenly shy.

ALEXANDRA *(cont.)* How are you?

TATIANA Hello, Varenka.

LIUBOV We've missed you horribly.

VARENKA Oh, so have I! I've told Dyakov I'm going to come back again and stay for a few months.

TATIANA Until the—?

Alexandra claps her hand over Tatiana's mouth.

ALEXANDRA We don't know, we don't know!

The four sisters collapse together in tearful happy embraces.

Alexander appears on the verandah, fulminating.

ALEXANDER   Did you know about this?

TATIANA AND ALEXANDRA   No!

LIUBOV   About what?

ALEXANDER   Where is he? Damnable boy! Egotist! Wait till he's got children of his own. Oh, congratulations, my dear—Dyakov told me—very good.

DYAKOV, *aged about fifty, a cavalry officer, smoking a celebratory cigar, joins Alexander. His three sisters-in-law respond.*

SISTERS   Congratulations! How lovely! We can't wait! . . .

DYAKOV   I'm the happiest man in the world.

ALEXANDER (*resuming*)   Your brother's going to end up in the Peter-and-Paul Fortress under lock and key!

He goes back inside with Dyakov.

LIUBOV (*to Tatiana*)   What did she say?

Michael, keeping a canny eye out for Alexander, appears from near the house smoking a cigar. He is in uniform.

MICHAEL   Have you heard? Wonderful news. I'm going to be an uncle! Well, of course you have.

LIUBOV   Congratulations.

MICHAEL   Thank you, thank you. I haven't got used to it yet. Yes, it's an amazing feeling, an uncle at last. Congratulations to you, too, Varenka. And Dyakov, of course. Another cavalry officer! Behind my back while I was serving my country.

TATIANA Father's looking for you.

VARENKA (*in regard to Alexander*) What have you been up to?

MICHAEL What have *you* been up to is more like it.

Varenka, speechless for a moment, turns to flee in tears. Liubov, with a reproachful look at Michael, leaves with Varenka—further into the garden.

MICHAEL (*cont.*) (*watching them go*) Illusion . . . it's only illusion. Well . . . can I have my letter back?

ALEXANDRA It's not yours, it's to us.

MICHAEL The letter is to you but the paper and ink were only on loan.

Alexandra crumples the letter and throws it at him.

ALEXANDRA There you are, keep it! Natalie Beyer is a pompous impertinent little snot and she's going to get what for!

TATIANA Go to her, then—it's obvious you care more for her than us, she understands you so well.

MICHAEL So in general you disagree with her analysis.

ALEXANDRA In general she can go and boil her head. And you should know better. She isn't even pretty.

TATIANA Yes, she is. (*Tatiana bursts into tears.*)

MICHAEL Tata, Tata, my beloved, don't cry. I renounce all love except pure philosophical love, your love, the love I have for my sisters. The so-called love of talking animals removes people two by two from the only possibility of happiness, which is the communion of beautiful souls.

TATIANA No, no—we don't mind—you'll meet somebody one day.

MICHAEL It's not for me. Don't be angry with Natalie. She thinks it's your fault that I couldn't . . . that I can't be . . .

ALEXANDRA What?

Alexander, emerging, sees them from the verandah.

ALEXANDER No spunk, simple as that! (*Explains.*) Your brother's an army deserter!

MICHAEL (*casually*) Oh yes, I've resigned my commission.

ALEXANDER He's refusing to return to duty.

MICHAEL On grounds of ill health, Papa. I'm sick of the Army.

ALEXANDER No discipline, that's the problem!

MICHAEL No, it's *riddled* with discipline, *that's* the problem. That and Poland.

ALEXANDER Come inside, sir!

MICHAEL Poland is simply impossible.

Alexander goes in. The girls escort Michael, chattering anxiously.

TATIANA AND ALEXANDRA Resigned from the Army? You haven't! Oh, Michael, won't you be in trouble? What did they say? What did you . . . ?

MICHAEL 'March here, march there, present arms, where's your cap?'—you've no idea, the whole Army's obsessed with playing at soldiers . . .

They go together into the house.

AUTUMN 1835

Liubov and Varenka 'return' to the garden. Varenka is eight months pregnant. Liubov has a book.

LIUBOV   That was the last time everything was all right, in the time of Baron Renne. When we were all on the same side in everything, the way we'd always been. I would rather have married him if I'd known what terrible rows . . .

VARENKA *(lightly)*   Where was Michael when *I* needed saving? But Dyakov's all right, if it wasn't for . . . and that's not his fault, we can't all be philosophers when it comes to love. This has been a godsend, even the feeling sick part, not having to want to. Did you ever want to with Baron Renne?

LIUBOV   Oh no!

VARENKA   It's the spurs.

LIUBOV   Oh, Varenka.

They hug each other, laughing and weeping.

LIUBOV *(cont.)* *(Pause.)*   Do you think it's ever wonderful, apart from in stories, like in George Sand?

VARENKA   I wouldn't mind it with . . . Eugene Onegin!

LIUBOV   Yes!

They giggle complicitly.

LIUBOV *(cont.)*   Don't you think Nicholas Stankevich looks like Onegin ought to look?

VARENKA   Perhaps I'll meet my Onegin and run off with him.

LIUBOV (*shocked*)   Varenka! (*Pause.*) Anyway, in Pushkin's story, Tatiana stayed with her husband.

VARENKA   That's because she hadn't read George Sand.

LIUBOV   Yes!

VARENKA   To follow our heart wherever it leads us! To love where we may, whomever we may, to let love be our guide to the greater good!

LIUBOV (*Pause.*)   Sand doesn't tell you the things you want to know, though.

VARENKA   I'll tell you if you want.

LIUBOV   No. Well . . . go on then.

VARENKA   You have to ask.

LIUBOV   I can't.

VARENKA   Remember that time the tinker's jackass got into Betsy's paddock?

LIUBOV   Yes!

VARENKA   Like that, only you're lying on your back.

LIUBOV   Oh . . .

VARENKA   Not as big as that.

They laugh complicitly, through Liubov's confusion. Voices are heard within.

LIUBOV   Is that them? Don't look.

Michael is seen indoors, with NICHOLAS STANKEVICH, a beautiful dark-haired young man aged twenty-two. Michael, hearing the laughter, has gone to the window.

MICHAEL   It's Liubov. Varenka's with her.

STANKEVICH The laughter of women is like the spiritual communion of angels. Women are holy beings. For me, love is a religious experience.

VARENKA I don't think he does it.

LIUBOV Varenka! . . . (*anxiously*) Don't you?

VARENKA Nicholas Stankevich is keeping himself for you. The next step has got him baffled. But Michael says Nicholas has the most brilliant mind in the Philosophical Circle, so perhaps an idea will come to him . . . Ask him if he'd like you to show him the . . .

LIUBOV The what? The fishpond? (*suddenly*) Promise not to tell—I've got his keepsake!

Liubov retrieves from 'next to her heart' the keepsake, a miniature penknife, an inch or two long when folded.

VARENKA Well, why didn't you say!

LIUBOV (*laughing, embarrassed*) Right next to my heart!

VARENKA What did he give you? His penknife?

LIUBOV Oh, no . . . he didn't give it, I . . . (*in tears*) I'm a fool. Natalie was just making mischief.

Liubov makes to flee. Varenka catches her and hugs her.

Indoors Michael and Stankevich, pupil and guide, sit at the table with their collection of hooks.

STANKEVICH Schelling's God is the cosmos, the totality of Nature struggling towards consciousness, and Man is as far as the struggle has got, with the animals not too far behind, vegetables somewhat lagging, and rocks nowhere as yet. Do we believe this? Does it matter? Think of it as a poem or a picture. Art doesn't have to be true like a theorem. It can be true in other ways. This truth says the universe is all of a oneness, not just a lot of bits which happen to be lying around together. In other words, it says there is a meaning to it all, and Man is where the meaning begins to show. How do we get the rest of the meaning? Schelling says: by unlocking our innermost being. By letting the meaning flow through us. This is morality. Kant says: but morality has no meaning unless we are free to choose, so it follows that we are the only government of our real lives, the ideal is to be discovered in *us,* not in some book of social theory written by a Frenchman. Idealism—the self—the autonomous will—is the mark of God's faith in his creations. Well, who'd have thought that God's chosen people would turn out to be the Germans?

In the garden, Liubov and Varenka have settled on the bench. Varenka stands up decisively.

VARENKA I'm going to ask him.

LIUBOV No!

VARENKA Well, stay here where he can see you reading.

LIUBOV I won't *fling* myself at him.

VARENKA Loosen your hair a little.

LIUBOV Varenka, don't . . .

VARENKA I won't, I won't.

Varenka leaves. Liubov sits and opens her book.

STANKEVICH The inner life is more real, more complete, than what we call reality—which has no meaning independent of my observing it. (*pausing to look*) I look out of the window. What is my thought experience? A garden. Trees. Grass. A young woman in a chair reading a book. I think: if there were no chair she would fall on the grass. If there were no book she would not be reading. Now the young woman touches her hair where it's come undone. How can we be sure there is a world of phenomena, a woman reading in a garden? Perhaps the only thing that's real is my sensory experience, which has the *form* of a woman reading—in a universe which is in fact empty! But Kant says no—I cannot have the experience without there being something out there to *cause* the experience. In fact, a woman reading. Am I, therefore, no more than an instrument for registering the phenomenal world of appearances, a woman now closing her book and standing up? But again Kant says—no! Because what I perceive as reality includes concepts *which I cannot experience through the senses.* Time and space. Cause and effect. Relations between things. These concepts already exist in my mind, I must use them to make sense of what I observe. And thus my existence is necessary to a complete description of reality. Without me there is something wrong with this picture. The trees, the grass, the woman are merely—oh, she's coming! (*nervously*) She's coming in here!—I say, don't leave!—where are you going?

MICHAEL Father's looking for me anyway . . . (*gloomily*) I've had to ask him to settle a few debts here and there in the world of appearances, so now he's been busy getting me a job.

Liubov enters from the garden, with her book.

LIUBOV Oh—Michael!—(*noticing Stankevich*) Excuse me—

MICHAEL Nobody seems to understand Stankevich and I are engaged in a life-or-death struggle over material forces to unite our spirit with the Universal—and he has to go back to Moscow tomorrow! (*as Liubov makes to leave*) No, it doesn't matter now. (*to Stankevich*) The Provincial Governor is father's friend, so it follows that I should have an inky job in the civil service, and think myself lucky after my distinguished career in the military.

LIUBOV   You'll only be in Tver, we'll see you often.

MICHAEL   Alas, it is not to be. Nicholas and I intend to go to Berlin, to the fountainhead.

LIUBOV   But how will you live?

MICHAEL   Oh, I can teach . . . mathematics—I don't know, what does it matter? (*earnestly*) You see, Liubov, I'm one of those who are born for their time. I will do such things I know not, but I must sacrifice everything to that sacred purpose, to strengthen my resolve until I can say, 'Whatever I want, that's what God wants.' (*leaving, airily*) I'll explain it all to Father.

Michael goes out. Stankevich is at a loss, Liubov no less so. Stankevich tidies up his books. Presently there are faintly heard the sounds of a gigantic row from a distant room. It goes on for some time, then stops. Liubov is on the point of speaking when the door is flung open and Tatiana and Alexandra rush in speaking over each other.

TATIANA AND ALEXANDRA   Oh, Liubov!—Did you hear? Michael and Papa—Oh!—Sorry!—It's nothing!—

They are hardly in before they're out. Stankevich is about to speak when Varvara hurries into the room.

VARVARA (*without pausing, to Liubov*)   Now he thinks he's God!

Varvara crosses the room and leaves. Stankevich loses his nerve and makes to leave.

LIUBOV So you're going to Moscow tomorrow.

STANKEVICH Yes. (*Blurts.*) It's a long time since you came to the Philosophical Circle. We miss the . . . feminine viewpoint.

LIUBOV (*haplessly*) Doesn't Natalie Beyer still go?

STANKEVICH (*mistaking her, coldly*) I . . . I understand your meaning. . . .

LIUBOV (*panicking miserably*) I didn't mean any meaning!

Stankevich hastily starts gathering his books. Liubov snatches one up at random.

LIUBOV (*cont.*) May I borrow this? To read. (*She examines the title.*) Grundlegung zur Metaphysik der Sitten. Is it good?

STANKEVICH It's in German.

LIUBOV *Ich weiss.* [I know.]

STANKEVICH Yes . . . yes, of course, if you wish. But you have a book. Is it philosophy?

LIUBOV No. I don't know. It's only a novel, by George Sand.

STANKEVICH The philosopher of love.

LIUBOV Yes, she says love is the highest good.

STANKEVICH Perhaps in France. Kant says the only good actions are those performed out of a sense of duty, not from instinct . . . like passion or desire . . .

LIUBOV So to act out of love can never be good?

STANKEVICH In the sense that you cannot take moral credit from it. Because you are really pleasing yourself.

LIUBOV   Even if it gives happiness to another?

STANKEVICH   Yes. Consequences don't come into it.

LIUBOV   And to act out of a sense of duty, even if it leads to unhappiness . . . ?

STANKEVICH   Is a moral action, yes.

LIUBOV (*timidly*)   In Germany.

STANKEVICH (*insistently*)   In the system of Kant a man is judged only by his intention.

LIUBOV (*still timidly*)   A *fool* can mean well.

STANKEVICH (*bursts out*)   And usually does! How was I to know that Natalie Beyer mistook my intentions? I only talked to her about philosophy!

LIUBOV   Yes. Only another fool would make that mistake.

She takes the little penknife from her pocket and holds it out to him.

LIUBOV (*cont.*)   I found this. I think it's your penknife.

STANKEVICH   Mine? No, it's not mine.

LIUBOV   Oh. Didn't you lose one?

STANKEVICH   No. (*Pause.*) Perhaps I should have one.

LIUBOV   Yes. Well, you can . . .

Michael bursts in with a bulging satchel over each shoulder.

MICHAEL   We're leaving!

He puts one satchel over Stankevich's shoulder, as Tatiana, Alexandra and Varenka rush in, talking over each other, while Michael gathers up the books, thrusting them at Stankevich.

VARENKA Michael—just for *once*—

TATIANA Don't go, don't go! What will you do? We'll all beg Father—

STANKEVICH What happened?

MICHAEL *Dahin! Dahin! Lass uns ziehn!* [There, there lies our path!]

ALEXANDRA When will you come back?

MICHAEL Never!

Michael starts pulling Stankevich to the garden.

MICHAEL (*cont.*) I've sent Semyon to hold the mail—

Varvara rushes into the room and joins the rout.

VARVARA You have broken your father's heart! When you get to Moscow, go to Pliva's and tell them to send another metre of the grey silk—will you remember?—the grey silk!

Michael, Stankevich, Varvara, Varenka, Tatiana, Alexandra, and now also two SERFS with bits of baggage, stream across the garden amid general lamentation and rebuke.

MICHAEL I don't need parents! I renounce them! They don't exist! They'll never see me again!

The chaotic exodus moves out of sight and then out of earshot. Liubov, alone, sits down at the table. Alexander enters the room, sees her, and sits next to her. As would have been indicated in the previous scene, Alexander has been aging noticeably since we first saw him only two and a half years earlier.

ALEXANDER I myself am a Doctor of Philosophy. My dissertation was on worms. We did not chatter about some inner life. Philosophy does not consist in spinning words like tops till the colours run together and one will do as well as another. Philosophy consists in moderating each life so that many lives will fit together with as much liberty and justice as will keep them together—and not so much as will make them fly apart, when the harm will be the greater. I am not a despot. For Michael to have fallen in with my wishes would have been praiseworthy and, yes, philosophically fitting; for me to fall in with his would be absurd and despicable. My son tells me I persecuted you, in the time of your betrothal. He says I persecuted you—you, my beloved daughter. Can it be true?

Liubov weeps into his breast.

ALEXANDER (*cont.*)   How the world must have been changing while I was holding it still.

Spring 1836

Garden and interior.

A Nurse (a serf) pushes a baby carriage with a crying infant across the garden, away from the house, going out of view.

Alexander and Liubov are where they were, her head against his breast, his fingers searching her hair.

LIUBOV   Ooh, lovely, you can scratch a bit harder.

Varenka enters from the further garden carrying the mewling baby, with Tatiana pushing the empty pram and Alexandra dancing attendance, all of them making for indoors.

ALEXANDRA   You don't have to go in, we'll tell you if anybody comes.

VARENKA   Little greedy boy, aren't you?

ALEXANDRA Will you let me have a little go, Varenka?

TATIANA Don't be stupid! How can you . . .

ALEXANDRA Stupid yourself, I mean just to see what it feels like.

Varenka takes the baby into the house. Alexandra goes with her. Tatiana takes a basket of gooseberries from the pram, then notices pipe smoke coming from the hammock. She approaches the hammock stealthily. Varvara enters the room with a jug.

VARVARA Where did Michael go? He bothers Masha to make lemonade and then disappears.

LIUBOV He's in the garden, working.

VARVARA We should light a candle.

From a distance, Tatiana lobs a gooseberry into the hammock without result.

LIUBOV He brought home a magazine with an article he wrote.

ALEXANDER The final straw. Journalism.

VARVARA What's all this?

ALEXANDER She's got nits.

LIUBOV No, I haven't.

ALEXANDER I can see their little arms and legs.

Liubov hastily disengages from him.

LIUBOV You couldn't see them if they were as big as ladybirds.

VARVARA What magazine?

24

ALEXANDER *The Universal Transcendent and Absolute Idiot.* My nurse washed my hair in water strained through the ashes from the kitchen stove—deadly for nits.

LIUBOV I haven't got nits! (*giving the magazine to Varvara*) The *Telescope!*

ALEXANDER He hasn't written it, he only translated it—another German windbag.

LIUBOV Well, he got paid, thirty roubles! And he has a commission to translate a whole history book.

A book and a pencil are flung out of the hammock. Michael sits up, smoking a pipe.

TATIANA The first goosegogs.

MICHAEL Thank you. Oh, Tata, you've made me happy again!

They embrace. He pulls her into the hammock, laughing. They remain visible. She feeds him a gooseberry.

MICHAEL (*cont.*) You read my article? I got led astray by Schelling. He tried to make the Self part of nature—but now *Fichte* shows that nature is simply non-Self!—there is nothing but Self—the soul must become its own object!

VARVARA (*laying the magazine aside*) Well, I wouldn't give thirty kopecks for it.

ALEXANDER After all these years, intellectual soul mates.

Tatiana's laughter attracts Varvara to the window.

VARVARA You all get happy and silly when Michael's home, until disaster strikes. Tatiana had a letter for the post boy, to Count Sollogub.

ALEXANDER I don't know why he had to run away to Moscow in the first place.

VARVARA A really thick envelope, she must have written him pages and pages.

LIUBOV Don't get your hopes up there, *Maman*.

VARVARA Why, what has she told you?

MICHAEL I heard Sollogub was a fop.

TATIANA Yes—not like you.

ALEXANDER He got homesick, you see. His friend Stankevich has gone coughing to the Caucasus. That doesn't sound good. He's asked another friend to come and stay in the summer, a critic.

VARVARA What sort of critic?

ALEXANDER Very shy and nervous, he says—not like that desperado Stankevich—we have to be kind to him, he's only a country doctor's son, poor as a mouse.

VARVARA Well, that's no use. (*to Liubov*) You don't mean she was sending the Count's letters back?

LIUBOV *You* must ask her, Mother. (*Liubov stands up abruptly and looks out at the garden.*)

MICHAEL I shall never doubt you again, Tata—or myself.

Tatiana lets herself down from the hammock.

TATIANA Well, your letter was horrible.

MICHAEL I was suffering, that's why.

She tips Michael out of the hammock. Liubov comes into the garden.

TATIANA   Liubov! Have you heard?

LIUBOV   There's lemonade.

MICHAEL (*cheerfully*)   I've discovered a new philosophy,
Liubov. Now I know where I was going wrong.

They all three go companionably to the house.

AUGUST 1836

Twilight and darkening.

*Alexander and Varvara remain. A doleful piano is heard in the
house. The room fills up with family—Alexandra, Tatiana, Liubov,
Michael—and* SERVANTS, *who bring lamps. The table is cleared
and dishes are set out, the lemonade jug passed round. Soup is
supped.*

VISSARION BELINSKY *appears from the shadows in the garden.
He is dressed in his scuffed and shabby best, and carries a valise. He
approaches the lighted window uncertainly.*

VARVARA   Where's Varenka?

The piano ceases.

LIUBOV   She's coming.

VARVARA   Why isn't she with her husband?

LIUBOV   *Maman!*

VARVARA   Or he with her, can anyone tell me?

ALEXANDER   Varvara, it's none of our business.

MICHAEL   Don't worry, I've got it in hand.

Alexander chokes on his soup. Dogs bark outside. Belinsky panics, retreats, falls over his valise. Servants come from the house. Michael comes into the garden. Meanwhile, Varenka enters and takes her place at the table. Inconspicuously, she lowers her eyes for a few moments in prayer before attending to her surroundings.

MICHAEL Belinsky!

VARVARA Is it his friend?

MICHAEL I thought you'd lost your nerve!—Did you walk from the posting station?

BELINSKY I'm sorry.

VARVARA What a time to arrive.

MICHAEL Give me that.

He gives the valise to a servant, who takes it into the house.

BELINSKY I knew it would be like this.

The sisters, except Varenka, steal glances through the window.

ALEXANDRA He looks peculiar.

LIUBOV But . . . I know him, he came to the Philosophical Circle.

MICHAEL (*entering with Belinsky*) It's Belinsky, he missed the pony trap.

Belinsky is twenty-five, not tall but stooped, with a hollow chest, a protruding shoulder blade, a pale, pinched face, and fair hair falling over his averted eyes.

ALEXANDER I am Michael's father.

BELINSKY Belinsky.

ALEXANDER   Come in, sit down!

MICHAEL   Sit there! Next to Alexandra.

Belinsky blindly sits on a lap, jumps up, knocks over a bottle, and stumbles to the inner door, escaping, followed hastily by Michael. Alexandra stifles a laugh unsuccessfully.

ALEXANDER   That's enough. It's nothing to laugh at. (*to Varvara*) Tell him it's all right . . .

Varvara follows Michael out. Alexandra can't contain her laughter.

ALEXANDER (*cont.*) (*angry*)   Leave the room, then, you can do without supper.

Alexandra leaves, still convulsed.

ALEXANDER (*cont.*)   There. Is anyone else not hungry?

Pause. Supper resumes in silence.

VARENKA   Yes, I'm not.

She gets up abruptly, crosses herself, and leaves.

LIUBOV   She's unhappy, Papa. Can I go to her?

ALEXANDER   I give up!

He puts down his spoon and stamps out. Liubov stands up to leave.

TATIANA (*intensely*)   Liubov . . . did you feel it?

LIUBOV   What?

TATIANA   That man . . . that man is greater than any of us, he's a greater man than Michael.

Liubov is impatient of the moment. She leaves.

Tatiana, left alone, sits back in her chair, and after a moment goes out to the garden, slowly crossing out of view.

AUTUMN 1836

Late afternoon on a nice autumn day.

A shrieking young woman, a house serf, runs across the garden pursued by Varvara, who is holding a garment and a garden cane with which she slashes at the woman in rage. They disappear from view.

Alexandra comes into view in the garden, followed by Belinsky with a fishing pole and a good-sized (five-pound) carp.

BELINSKY   Five hundred souls . . . ! A man with five hundred souls must have a good chance of salvation.

ALEXANDRA   Our forester Vasilly says the weather will change tomorrow, so we must all watch the sunset . . . He's nearly a hundred years old, that's how he knows.

BELINSKY   At the *Telescope,* we've got a manuscript that's been going from hand to hand for years . . . Nadezhdin, my editor, says if he can get it past the censor, it'll put the *Telescope* on the map, or finish us off with a bang . . . Anyway, it's all about how backward Russia is compared with Europe . . . the *rest* of Europe, sorry . . . but the author could have pointed out that in the matter of the ownership of human beings we were years ahead of America . . .

Belinsky leans the fishing pole against the wall. He takes a posy of wildflowers from inside his shirt, Alexandra pays no attention.

ALEXANDRA   You didn't say anything for weeks, and now whenever you say anything, you say anything.

She goes into the house. Belinsky, embarrassed by the flowers, guiltily throws them out of sight. He follows Alexandra indoors.

Michael, Varenka, Tatiana and Liubov appear in the garden. Michael has got the book which he threw out of the hammock, leafing through it in a cursory manner. Varenka is looking at a letter.

VARENKA I spent hours writing it. I don't want to he unfair to Dyakov. He's the baby's father, after all.

Tatiana takes the letter from her and looks at it.

MICHAEL Well, I'm its uncle. Anyway, Kant says relations are mental concepts. (*He manages to tear out a whole chunk of the book, handing the pages to Liubov.*) Here, you can have 'Charlemagne to the Hussite Rebellion.'

TATIANA (*returning the letter to Varenka*) What Michael says is, write to him that when you gave yourself to him, your body was just the phenomenal manifestation of the ego.

VARENKA He's a cavalry officer.

Michael hands another chunk of the book to Tatiana.

MICHAEL 'Maximilian the First to the Peace of Utrecht.'

TATIANA (*impatiently*) Oh, Michael!

MICHAEL It'll soon get done if we do a bit each. Strogonov keeps writing to ask for his four hundred roubles back.

He tears the remainder of the book in two and gives half to Varenka.

MICHAEL (*cont.*) 'Napoleon' . . . There was a letter from Nicholas, too—he thinks the same as me.

The young woman limps sobbing back to the house.

VARENKA Nicholas wants me to leave my husband?

MICHAEL Come back with me to Moscow next time, Liubov. He does like you.

LIUBOV Did he say so?

Alexander comes into the garden via the verandah with Belinsky and Alexandra.

TATIANA Vissarion!—Did you catch anything?

MICHAEL Of course he did—and what do you think he found inside it this time?

VARENKA Nothing. The carp fairy doesn't repeat herself.

MICHAEL Don't disappoint us, Belinsky. Was it a silver rouble you once gave to an old beggarwoman?

Varvara walks back across the garden, holding the garment.

VARVARA Stupid girl. Look at this—she hung out my skirt where the goat could chew the buttons.

ALEXANDER But can you live as the literary critic of the *Telescope?*

TATIANA You can if you're Vissarion, in one room over a blacksmith's.

The group position themselves, standing or sitting, towards the sunset.

MICHAEL The readers should see him—pacing and scribbling, swaddled in scarves and coughing, and throwing each page to the floor as he goes, with the anvil pounding below and the smell of soapsuds and wet washing from the laundry across the landing . . . (*giving Belinsky a letter*) You had a letter.

Michael's attitude to Belinsky has altered to condescension barely concealed. He is jealous.

VARVARA Above a blacksmith's? What a place to put a laundry!

ALEXANDRA Oh, Mother!

VARVARA Well, it is.

ALEXANDER Another sunset, another season nearer God . . .

LIUBOV You shouldn't be living next to all that steam and damp, it can't be good for you.

ALEXANDRA Have you met Pushkin, Vissarion?

Belinsky, having opened the letter, puts it in his pocket unread.

BELINSKY No. He's in St Petersburg.

ALEXANDRA How old is he?

ALEXANDER Too young for you.

Michael does an amused 'Ha ha' at Alexandra's expense.

ALEXANDER (*cont.*) (*to Belinsky*) In my opinion a man shouldn't get married until he's at least twice the age of his wife. I was forty-two and my . . .

ALEXANDRA (*chiming with him*) . . . forty-two and my wife was eighteen . . .

ALEXANDER Quite so.

ALEXANDRA (*pertly*) I'll wait for him, then.

BELINSKY But . . . the longer you wait . . .

ALEXANDER (*to Belinsky*) Waste of breath. (*to Alexandra*) What about Vyazemski? He had two horses shot from under him at Borodino, one easily forgives the poetry.

VARVARA Kozlov, Alexandra!

LIUBOV
 'Oh, where my aching heart relieve when grief assails me sore,

My friend who sleeps in the cold earth comes to my
aid no more!'

TATIANA How morbid. No, Baratynski! 'The Gipsy Girl.'

ALEXANDER Oh, dear. I appeal to our critic.

TATIANA Yes, the case requires a critic of literature.

They all look to Belinsky.

BELINSKY We have no literature.

Pause.

ALEXANDER Oh, well. I'll give Mr Pushkin my provisional
blessing, in the event that he survives his wife.

MICHAEL (*to Alexandra*) Pushkin never wrote a poem for you
like Vissarion . . . (*to Belinsky*) It's all right, it's not a secret,
we've all read it.

TATIANA I suppose you think we're terrible. Are you sorry
you came now?

BELINSKY No. It's like being in a dream . . . (*amazed*) and
you all live here! Lost objects from another life are restored
to you in the belly of a carp.

ALEXANDRA He says anything.

BELINSKY It's true, though.

TATIANA But how did the penknife get into the carp?

VARENKA Somebody threw it in the fishpond and the carp
saw it and just gobbled it up.

ALEXANDER (*in 'English'*)
'The moon is up and yet it is not night;
Sunset divides the sky with her . . .'
(*to Belinsky*) Do you read in English?

MICHAEL No, he doesn't.

TATIANA Vissarion's going to read us his new article—that's the most exciting thing that's happened at Premukhino, ever . . . To think, when it's published in the *Telescope,* and being read by hundreds of people . . . and we were there when it was being written, with ink from our old brass inkpot just as if it was an ordinary letter . . .

LIUBOV What is it about?

BELINSKY It's nothing, it's only a book review.

TATIANA It's about how we're stuck between the eighteenth and nineteenth centuries.

MICHAEL Well, Tatiana's in the know. Enlighten us, Belinsky.

BELINSKY I'll read it out after supper.

MICHAEL But I may have better things to do after supper.

VARENKA Who is stuck?

TATIANA Russia is. Stuck between dried-up old French reasoning and the new German thought which explains everything.

ALEXANDER Everyone knows that German thought is infinitely superior to French thought.

TATIANA Well, it is, isn't it, Vissarion?

MICHAEL Idealism is concerned with questions that lie outside reasoning, it's quite simple. Reason has triumphed over all the ancient problems of natural science, so the clever fools in France thought they could solve the problem of society—of morality, art—in the same way, by reason and experiment, as if God our Maker was a chemist, an astronomer, a clockmaker . . .

ALEXANDER (*losing patience*) God is all those things. That's the point!

Michael bows to patriarchal authority. Belinsky misses the warning.

BELINSKY No, the point is, the question 'how to make a clock' has the same answer for everybody.

The contradicting of Alexander disturbs everybody in different ways. Belinsky remains unaware.

BELINSKY (*cont.*) We can all be clockmakers, or astronomers. But if we all wanted to be Pushkin . . . if the question is, how do you make a poem by Pushkin?—or, what exactly makes one poem or painting or piece of music greater than another?—or, what is beauty? or liberty? or virtue?—if the question is, how should we live? . . . then reason gives no answer or different answers. So something is wrong. The divine spark in man is not reason after all, but something else, some kind of intuition or vision, perhaps like the moment of inspiration experienced by the artist . . .

MICHAEL *Dahin! Dahin! Lass uns ziehn!* (*He translates specifically for Belinsky, with malice aforethought.*) 'There, there lies our path,' Belinsky.

ALEXANDER (*courteously*) Ah, you don't read German yourself?

BELINSKY No.

ALEXANDER Ah. But you know French.

BELINSKY Well . . .

Alexandra sniggers quietly behind her hand.

TATIANA (*defending him*)   Vissarion wasn't allowed to finish university.

VARVARA   Why not?

LIUBOV   Mother . . .

VARVARA   Well, I was only asking.

TATIANA   He wrote a play against serfdom, that's why.

Pause. Varvara gets up on her dignity and goes into the house.

MICHAEL (*quietly, to Tatiana*)   Idiot.

ALEXANDER (*courteously, with restraint*)   My estate is of five hundred souls and I am not ashamed. The landowner is the protector of all who live on his land. Our mutual obligations are the foundation on which Holy Russia rests. In the way of life at Premukhino there is true liberty. I know about the other kind, if I may say so; I was in France when they had their Revolution.

BELINSKY (*embarrassed*)   Yes . . . yes . . . allow me to . . . My article is not about our liberties . . . of course. When was there ever such an article published in Russia? I write about literature.

MICHAEL   You said we had no literature.

BELINSKY   That's what I write. We haven't. We have a small number of masterpieces, how could we not, there are so many of us, a great artist will turn up from time to time in much smaller countries than Russia. But as a nation we have no literature because what we have isn't ours, it's like a party where everyone has to come dressed up as somebody else—Byron, Voltaire, Goethe, Schiller, Shakespeare and the rest . . . I am not an artist. My play was no good. I am not a poet. A poem can't be written by an act of will. When the rest of us are trying our hardest to be present, a real poet goes absent. We can watch him in the moment of creation, there he sits with the pen in his hand, not moving. When it moves, we've missed it. Where did he go in that moment? The meaning of art lies in the answer to that question. To discover it, to understand it, to know the difference between it happening and not happening, this is my whole purpose in life, and it is not a contemptible calling in our country where our liberties cannot be discussed because we have none, and science or politics can't be discussed for the same reason. A critic does double duty here. If something true can be understood about art, something will be understood about liberty, too, and science and politics and history—because everything in the universe is unfolding together with a purpose of which mine is a part. You are right to laugh at me because I don't know German or French. But the truth of idealism would be plain to me if I had heard one sentence of Schelling shouted through my window by a man on a galloping horse. When philosophers start talking like architects, get out while you can, chaos is coming. When they start laying down rules for beauty, blood in the streets is from that moment inevitable. When reason and measurement are made authorities for the perfect society, seek sanctuary among the cannibals . . . Because the answer is not out there like America waiting for Columbus, the same answer for everybody forever. The universal idea speaks through humanity itself, and differently through each nation in each stage of its history. When the inner life of a nation speaks through the unconscious creative spirit of its artists, for generation after generation—then you have a national literature. That's why we have none. Look at us!— a gigantic child with a tiny head stuffed full of idolatry for everything foreign . . . and a huge inert body abandoned to its own muck, a continent of vassalage and superstition, an Africa of know-nothing have-nothings without a notion of a better life, or the wit to be discontented drunk or sober, that's your Russia, held together by police informers and fourteen ranks of uniformed flunkeys—how can we have a literature? Folk tales and foreign models, that's our lot, swooning over our imitation Racines and Walter Scotts— our literature is nothing but an elegant pastime for the upper classes, like dancing or cards. How did it happen? How did this disaster befall us? Because we were never trusted to grow up, we're treated like children and we deserve to be treated like children—flogged for impertinence, shut into cupboards for naughtiness, sent to bed without supper and not daring even to dream of the guillotine . . .

Long before this, Belinsky's speech has become progressively agitated, fervid, louder. Alone among his mesmerised family, Alexander makes to interrupt.

BELINSKY (*cont.*)   Yes—I've got off my track, hell and damnation . . . excuse me . . . it's always happening to me! . . . I forget what I'm trying to say—I'm sorry, I'm sorry . . . (*Belinsky makes to leave, but turns back.*) Every work of art is the breath of a single eternal idea. That's it. Forget the rest. Every work of art is the breath of a single eternal idea breathed by God into the inner life of the artist. That's where he went. (*He starts to go and comes back.*) We will have our literature. What kind of literature and what kind of life is the same question. Our external life is an insult. But we have produced Pushkin and now Gogol. Excuse me, I don't feel well.

This time he goes into the house. After a moment, Tatiana jumps up and follows him.

VARENKA (*Pause.*) Who's Gogol . . . ?

ALEXANDER We missed the sun going down. (*to Michael*) If Mr Belinsky is a literary critic, so was Robespierre.

Alexander goes angrily indoors. The baby, a year old, is heard crying. Varenka stands up.

ALEXANDRA (*eagerly*) Can I come?

VARENKA I'm going to write my letter again.

Varenka and Alexandra go indoors.

LIUBOV Yes . . . will you take me to Moscow with you when Nicholas comes back from the Caucasus?

MICHAEL (*cries out*) Oh, Liubov! Where can I turn?

He starts weeping, and walks away. Liubov follows him into the further garden.

LIUBOV What is it?—what has happened?

MICHAEL None of it's any use—the outer world worms itself into my heart like a serpent!

Belinsky comes out onto the verandah, his letter in his hand.

BELINSKY O my prophetic soul!—The *Telescope* has been banned! Closed down! They've arrested Nadezhdin!

MICHAEL (*ironically*) Illusion!—It's only illusion—

BELINSKY (*bewildered*) No . . . the police have searched my room. I have to get back to Moscow.

MICHAEL Yes—we must get out—out!—to Moscow!

He leaves. Belinsky goes back indoors.

LIUBOV Moscow . . . !

She follows Michael out.

A gunshot disturbs the crows in the wintry garden . . . overlapping the next scene.

A sudden wail of grief sounds out from inside the house.

JANUARY 1837

Interior. Alexandra is in an attitude of romantic despair, clutching a letter of several pages. Tatiana hurries into the room, followed by Varenka.

ALEXANDRA Tata . . . Liubov's had a letter from Nicholas.

TATIANA Let me see.

Alexandra flutters the letter, swooning. Tatiana takes it and starts to read, passing each page to Varenka to read.

VARENKA Michael's written, too.

ALEXANDRA (*operatically*) They took Pushkin back to his house and he lingered between life and death all the next day.

The three sisters congregate at a chaise longue where Liubov is lying, propped up by pillows. Varenka takes a letter from her pocket and gives it to Liubov.

VARENKA From Michael. (*tenderly*) How are you feeling?

ALEXANDRA Can I see?

Liubov starts reading Michael's letter, passing pages to Alexandra, while the remainder of the first letter—from Stankevich—passes from Tatiana to Varenka. Alexandra passes pages of Michael's letter to Tatiana, who returns them to Varenka. Varenka returns Stankevich's pages to Liubov. Meanwhile, as the pages pass from hand to hand:

TATIANA His wife killed him!—as surely as if she fired the shot!

ALEXANDRA It's just like in the story—perhaps they were friends like Onegin and Lensky.

TATIANA That's stupid—Onegin wasn't the one killed!

ALEXANDRA Stupid yourself!—he might have been.

TATIANA But he wasn't—and Pushkin *was*.

VARENKA How like Nicholas.

LIUBOV What's like Nicholas?

VARENKA Pushkin is killed in a duel, and somehow it's all about the tragedy of a woman marrying unwisely. Nicholas is always putting you off between the lines, like when he went to see *Hamlet* and it was all Ophelia's fault . . .

Tatiana and Alexandra at once abandon their squabble, alarmed.

ALEXANDRA AND TATIANA Michael says—Yes, Michael—

VARENKA (*bursts out*) I don't care what Michael says! (*She starts to cry.*) Michael calls my husband an animal. That's what he says to *me*. It's not right. Dyakov's done nothing wrong by normal people's standards. Everything's my fault. I'm going to beg his forgiveness.

Varenka would leave, but Liubov clasps her, also in tears.

LIUBOV Oh, Varenka, Varenka . . . and you sacrificed yourself for me . . . (*against Varenka's protest*) Yes—your marriage in exchange for mine, that's why Father gave in.

TATIANA (*tearfully, insisting*) Michael says Nicholas's love for Liubov has transformed his inner life.

ALEXANDRA (*likewise*) He says Liubov is Nicholas's ideal.

VARENKA (*shouts*) Go away! Go off to bed!

Tatiana and Alexandra are shocked into compliance.

ALEXANDRA (*leaving*) What did *we* do wrong?

They leave.

LIUBOV Don't you believe he loves me, Varenka?

VARENKA I wasn't there. What did you do, in Moscow?

LIUBOV We played duets on the piano.

VARENKA Well, that's something.

LIUBOV He wouldn't have asked me to write to him if . . .

VARENKA Then why doesn't he propose to you instead of lecturing you like a German?

LIUBOV He's going home to ask his father . . .

VARENKA And then he's going abroad!

LIUBOV He has to go, he's ill, he has to go to the spas.

VARENKA Why can't he marry you and take you with him? You need to go to the spas just as much as he does.

LIUBOV What do you mean?

VARENKA You know you do.

Liubov pulls away from her in distress, struggling.

LIUBOV   I don't, I don't! Don't say that!

Liubov goes into a coughing fit, breathless.

VARENKA (*embracing her*)   Liuba . . . Liuba . . . I'm sorry . . .
ssh . . . there, there, my lamb, I'm sorry for all the things I
said. You'll be well and Nicholas will come back and marry
you . . . I know he will.

SPRING 1838

*A bonfire blazes in the garden just out of plain sight. A Serf goes to
the fire with an armful of dead wood. A House Serf crosses from the
house, bringing provisions, utensils, folding chairs, cushions, etc.
Varvara comes from the direction of the picnic, folding up a lace bed-
cover. Tatiana comes from the house, hurrying and in a festive mood,
with a long-handled warming pan.*

VARVARA   Is Liubov ready?

TATIANA   She's coming. Her carriage awaits!

VARVARA   What are you doing with that? You'll burn the
handle.

TATIANA   No, I won't. It's the very thing. What's Michael
doing?

VARVARA   Explaining something to Father.

TATIANA   Oh, no!

*Tatiana goes out to the fire. A Serf Girl, she of the goat-chewed
buttons, comes from the house with a rolled-up carpet. Passing her,
Varvara casually boxes her ear.*

VARVARA   The lace tablecloth—*tablecloth!*—not the coverlet off my bed!

Varvara goes into the house. The girl follows Tatiana out. Alexander and Michael come from the further garden, not from the bonfire, with bunches of lilies and white flowers they have picked. Alexander also has a periodical, the Moscow Observer, *which has a green cover.*

MICHAEL   Agriculture? I'd rather kill myself than study agriculture. But after three years in Berlin I'd be qualified for a professorship. I am prepared for it. I was on the wrong track with Fichte, I admit it—Fichte was trying to get rid of objective reality, but *Hegel* shows that reality can't be ignored, on the contrary, reality is the interaction of the inner and outer worlds, you see, Father, and harmony is achieved by suffering through the storms of contradiction between the two—as I have suffered: that's why I have never been more in harmony with myself than now, that's why I am worthy of your trust.

Alexander gives Michael the magazine.

ALEXANDER   You've changed windbags, that's all. It's well and good for Robespierre to be editor of the new Moscow Monthly Windbaggery, I congratulate him, the first middle-class intellectual in Russia and it can't be helped, but a gentleman has a duty to look after his estate.

Varenka comes out of the house with two bottles of red wine and a small basket of lemons and spices.

MICHAEL   Belinsky is not one of us, I agree. In fact, I have broken off relations with him. He's turned out to be a complete egoist. But my estate is self-fulfilment and the future of philosophy in Russia.

VARENKA The musicians are ready.

ALEXANDER We've got the flowers.

Michael follows Alexander indoors.

MICHAEL Two thousand a year from my inheritance, even fifteen hundred, Father . . . I'm desperate . . .

Varenka continues towards the fire and is met by Tatiana, who takes the bottles and basket from her.

TATIANA A *fête champêtre*! How does she look?

VARENKA Beautiful! Like a bride. Alexandra's doing her hair.

TATIANA Oh, it's going to be lovely. Get Michael away from Father before he . . .

VARENKA Yes!—Yes! . . .

Tatiana hurries back to the fire. Varenka hurries towards the house—too late. In the house, Alexander is heard raising his voice—'No! Enough!'—and he enters the room with Michael dogging him. They no longer have the flowers. Varenka pauses outside, aware of them.

ALEXANDER (*angrily*) Your own life you have wasted at every turn, and sponged off friends and strangers until your name is a byword for bad faith and discounted bills. You have turned your sisters' faces away from the light of parental love, and poisoned their minds with liberal sophistries dressed up as idealism. With your meddling, you've broken their lives like a spoiled child smashing his breakfast egg to annoy his nurse. Liubov would have been long married to a nobleman who loved her. Instead, she is betrothed by permanent correspondence with an invalid who evidently can't drink Russian water even if it meant he could set eyes on his future wife. Tatiana you defended from her only suitor as though he were a Turk intent on stealing her maidenhead.

His speech has carried him to the verandah, from where Varenka is conveniently included in his tour d'horizon.

ALEXANDER *(cont.)*   Yes, and you incited Varenka to leave her husband whom she freely chose, and incited her again when she tried to make it up with him, until she was half out of both her minds, and now she, too, must go and drink the amazing German tapwater with her son. Dyakov is a sainted fool to let her go, but now that I see you have plotted this together—

Varenka attempts denial. Michael flings himself into a chair and buries his head in his hands. Alexander continues on his way towards the fire.

ALEXANDER *(cont.)*   —I'll be damned if I pay for any more of your wilfulness. You will not go to Berlin. That is my last word.

Alexander leaves. Varenka goes inside to Michael.

VARENKA   Why did you have to ask him *today*?

MICHAEL   Nicholas has written. It's bad news.

VARENKA *(Pause.)*   Tell me.

MICHAEL   He can't lend me any more money. You'll have to go on your own.

Alexandra puts her head in the door.

ALEXANDRA *(excitedly)*   Ready!

She disappears. Varenka starts to laugh in hysterical relief.

47

MICHAEL   What is to be done?

VARENKA   Well, we mustn't let it show. Everything must be happy.

Varenka leaves.

Turgenev enters the garden: an overlap with the next scene.

MICHAEL   *Dahin! Dahin! Lass uns ziehn!*

He follows Varenka out.

Autumn 1841

IVAN TURGENEV *is joined in the garden by Tatiana. He is twenty-three and well over six feet tall, with a surprisingly light, high voice.*

TURGENEV   Yes, twice, three times counting in his coffin . . . The first time, I didn't know it was Pushkin. He was leaving a party at Pletnyov's as I arrived, he'd already got his hat and coat on. The second time was at a concert at the Engelhardt Hall. He was leaning against a doorway, glancing around with a sort of scowl. I'm afraid I stared at him and he caught me and walked off looking vexed. I felt misunderstood, but I was flattering myself. He had more important things to vex him, it was just a few days before the duel. Well . . . I was a boy—nearly five years ago now, I was eighteen—and Pushkin was a demigod to me.

TATIANA   Are you a writer?

TURGENEV   No. But I thought I was. (*He 'shoots' at birds flying over. Laughs.*) I'm a sportsman. (*Pause.*) But I'd still like to write a decent poem one day. Tomorrow, for example. It's lovely here. I'd like to stay.

TATIANA (*too quickly*)   You can. (*Pause.*) Michael's letter said, 'Ivan Turgenev is my brother . . .'

TURGENEV   Michael described every inch of Premukhino . . . strolling down Unter den Linden to our favourite café. He talks about home all the time.

TATIANA   When he was here he talked about nothing but going to Berlin. Nicholas Stankevich was there, and Michael schemed and begged for years . . . and then when he got to Berlin at last, he heard Nicholas had died a month before in Italy.

TURGENEV   Yes, what a cure that turned out to be. It makes one angry, a death like that. Beside it, Pushkin's death is a comedy.

Tatiana gasps, distressed.

TURGENEV (*cont.*)   An absurdity. If we weren't in tears, it would be sidesplitting. No other social class but ours could count it natural behaviour, to march grimly into the snow with loaded pistols and bang away because according to some anonymous lampoon a woman who once stirred your blood, and now only irritates you, is being kept occupied by someone as yet in the first stage of discovery. If we lived somewhere like . . . the Sandwich Islands, it would be the seducer who gets the sniggers while the husband hands out cigars to his friends . . . (*Pause.*) But the White Death that slips into the breast of the young and brave, blind to sense as a slow-worm, and makes itself at home, feeding on blood and breath . . . How do they like it now, those fine catchwords which sound even nobler in German?—the Universal, the Eternal, the Absolute, the Transcendent? How they must blush and shift about when they bump up against death by wasting and coughing—(*He realises that Tatiana is upset.*)—of course, of course—I'm so clumsy.

TATIANA I always think of Liubov at this time of day in the garden . . . Once, not long before she died, Michael made a bonfire, just over there in the copse, and we brought Liubov out in a carriage like a queen coming to the dance . . . and I mulled the wine in a warming-pan . . . !

The bonfire becomes audible, luciferous offstage.

Liubov, brought from bed, reclining in a bed made up on a cart, is drawn into view by Michael, Varenka and Alexandra, who are in high spirits, calling, 'Here she is! Careful, careful!', with Varvara keeping up and fussing over her. Liubov has a bouquet of the flowers picked by Alexander and Michael, which also decorate the cart. Two Serf Musicians accompany her. Alexander comes to meet the cart, with a glass in his hand.

ALEXANDER This way, this way! *Gluhwein!*

TATIANA It was the last time we were all together, and somehow we were happy! . . . even Varenka. She'd sent Dyakov away after one last effort to be his wife, and she was going to Germany with her son. It was Dyakov's final service.

The cart is pulled out of sight. Varenka hangs back. Michael comes to fetch her.

VARENKA But how will I live?

MICHAEL (*airily*) Oh, you can . . . give music lessons, I don't know, what does it matter?

They leave, laughing. The past fades.

TATIANA (*laughs to herself*)   The liberation of Varenka! She sold her bits of jewelry, and everyone was offering advice, Nicholas writing from Berlin . . .

TURGENEV   When I was in Rome I saw Nicholas and Varenka every day. Then, when I got back to Berlin, I had a letter from them, from Florence. He said he was doing better, and that he and Varenka were going to spend the summer by Lake Como. That was two weeks before he died in her arms. (*Pause.*) Yes . . . if you can't write a poem here, there's no hope. And not much if you can. (*responding to her glance*) At Premukhino the eternal, the ideal, seems to be in every breath around you, like a voice telling you how much more sublime is the unattainable, imagined happiness of the inner life, compared with the vulgar happiness of the crowd! And then you're dead. There's something missing in this picture. Stankevich was coming round to it, before the end. He said: 'For happiness, apparently, something of the real world is necessary.'

TATIANA   Would you like me to show you the—(*Stuck, she indicates vaguely.*)—fishpond?

TURGENEV   Yes, very much. (*He offers her his arm.*) Oh yes, we're all Hegelians now. 'What's rational is real, and what's real is rational.' But Nicholas brought me and Michael together. I've got written in my Hegel: 'Stankevich died June 24th 1840. I met Bakunin July 20th. In my life up to now, these are the only two dates I wish to remember.' (*Pause.*) No, it must have been the beginning of August. (*He 'shoots' a bird flying over.*) By the Western calendar. I always think—our situation in Russia isn't hopeless while we've still got twelve days to catch up.

They stroll away.

ACT TWO

Moscow. The Zoo Gardens, near the skating ground. A sunny day on the cusp of spring. Bandstand music at a distance. There are some tables and chairs set out on the grass in an area served by a waiter from offstage. NICHOLAS OGAREV, aged twenty-one, and NICHOLAS SAZONOV, aged twenty-two, are at a table. ALEXANDER HERZEN, aged twenty-two, is of the party but standing aside, eating an ice cream with a spoon. A fourth young man, Stankevich, aged twenty-one, is lying on the grass, unidentified as yet, apparently asleep with his cap over his face. Sazonov and Ogarev wear home-made 'French tricolour' neckerchiefs. Sazonov also wears a beret.

Liubov and Varvara, accompanying MRS BEYER, a well-to-do widow of about fifty, stroll into view.

HERZEN   What is wrong with this picture?

VARVARA   Varenka's engaged to an officer in the Cavalry . . . Nicholas Dyakov. He can't say boo to a goose—I don't think he's quite sure about that horse either—but otherwise very satisfactory. I was amazed Varenka accepted him without batting an eye, but thank God her future is settled. Unlike some.

MRS BEYER (*wagging her finger humorously at Liubov*)   You'll die an old maid. The Baron was a catch.

VARVARA   You see? You should listen to Mrs Beyer. But what's done is done, and it was Michael's doing, impossible boy, the sooner he's in the Army . . .

MRS BEYER   Children!

LIUBOV   There's your Natalie on the ice, Mrs Beyer.

They leave towards the skating ground.

HERZEN   You remember those puzzle pictures, when we
were children . . . there'd be a drawing with things wrong
in it, a clock with no hands, a shadow going the wrong
way, the sun and stars out at the same time . . . and it would
say, 'What is wrong with this picture?' . . . Someone sitting
next to you in class disappears overnight, nobody knows
anything. In the public gardens ice creams are eaten, in all
the usual flavours. What is wrong with this picture? The
Kritski brothers disappeared for insulting the Tsar's portrait,
Antonovich and his friends for forming a secret society,
meaning they met in somebody's room to read a pamphlet
you can buy on the street in Paris. Young men and women
are pairing off like swans on the skating ground. A crocodile
of Poles goes clanking by in leg-irons on the Vladimir road.
There is something wrong with this picture. Are you
listening? You're in the picture. Professor Pavlov, with a
twinkle in his eye, has taken to button-holing us with
philosophy—'You wish to understand the nature of reality?
Ah, but what do we mean by reality? By nature? What do
we mean by understand?' So that's philosophy, well, well,
and at Moscow University teaching philosophy is forbidden
as a threat to public order. Professor Pavlov's class is physics
and agriculture, it's only by centrifugal force that he goes
flying off from crop rotation to Schelling's philosophy of
nature . . . but what with Father Ternovsky substituting on
female diseases and the professor of gynaecology returning
the favour on the Immaculate Conception, nobody is the
wiser, so that's all right . . . (*looking out*) Ketscher!

NICHOLAS KETSCHER *enters, greeted by Ogarev and Sazonov. He is older, twenty-eight, and is something of an irascible uncle-figure to the younger men. He is tall and thin, with glasses, and wears a black cape.*

KETSCHER (*to Ogarev and Sazonov*)   Why are you dressed up like Frenchmen?

A Waiter enters with a tray of glasses of tea, which he puts on the table.

SAZONOV   Ah!—you noticed. Because France is the flower of civilisation, and also the home of revolution which will lop off the head of the flower.

KETSCHER (*to the Waiter as he leaves*)   Thank you . . . (*to Sazonov, nettled*) Then you might at least speak French in front of the waiter . . .

SAZONOV   *D'accord. Mille pardons!*

KETSCHER   It's a bit late now.

OGAREV   You're drunk, Sazonov.

SAZONOV   You sang 'The Marseillaise' outside the Maly Theatre.

OGAREV   I was drunk. I'm still drunk. (*He smashes his hand down on a glass, breaking it.*) Twenty-one and nothing done!

NICHOLAS POLEVOY *enters. He is thirty-eight but seems a generation older than the young men. He encounters the group on his stroll.*

POLEVOY   Gentlemen . . .

HERZEN   Mr Polevoy! . . . Good day to you!

POLEVOY   Good day . . . good day . . .

Polevoy raises his hat in general greeting, and, noticing the sleeping man, greets him also with a slight bow, raising Stankevich's cap slightly with his stick, to see his face.

POLEVOY Please don't disturb yourself. Ah, Mr Ketscher! I received your article. I liked it. If you wish me to make it public in the *Telegraph* . . . would you take some friendly advice? Before it goes to the censor . . . one or two expressions . . . allusions . . . if you'd allow me . . .

KETSCHER But it's an article about translating Shakespeare.

Polevoy smiles knowingly, steadfastly, until Ketscher concedes.

POLEVOY Will you trust me? Splendid. I'm delighted to have it . . . And what are those pretty scarves? Is it a club?

OGAREV It is.

Ogarev starts humming 'The Marseillaise,' Herzen and Sazonov joining in.

POLEVOY (*alarmed*) Now, stop—stop that! Please! Such foolishness!—and inconsiderate of my own position. Every issue of the *Telegraph* plays with fire—not my words; words spoken in the Third Section and carried back to me. They can close me down like that—(*snapping his fingers*)—for a word out of place, and send me to Siberia.

SAZONOV How long before it's our turn?

KETSCHER I suppose that depends on the waiter.

Sazonov thoughtfully puts his neckerchief in his pocket.

SAZONOV I think I'm sober.

OGAREV We made the scarves ourselves.

POLEVOY Well, of course you did, Mr Ogarev.

OGAREV Did you hear what happened? Five of our fellows arrested and sent into the Army. We got up a subscription for them . . . Ketscher and I were hauled in by Police General Lesovsky . . . our final warning, by the gracious clemency of Tsar Nicholas.

POLEVOY Well, thank God for His Majesty! I'm surprised at you, Mr Ketscher, in your station in life.

KETSCHER That's what Police General Lesovsky said.

POLEVOY (*stung*) That's unfair . . .

KETSCHER I'm a doctor, I'm not the Minister for Public Instruction.

POLEVOY Everyone knows where I stand. I've been a lone voice for reform . . . but reform from above, not revolution from below. What can a handful of students do? They destroyed themselves for nothing. Their names will be forgotten.

OGAREV Or live forever, perhaps.

HERZEN (*to Ogarev*) Are you writing a poem?

Ogarev jumps up, agitated by embarrassment, and starts to leave. He returns to the table to put some coins on it, then leaves again, but only as far as the next table, where he sits down with his back turned.

HERZEN (*cont.*) Sorry! (*confidentially*) He writes poetry . . . very good, too.

Stankevich rouses himself, ignoring everyone.

SAZONOV He's awake. Stankevich, tea has made a phenomenal appearance, look.

KETSCHER (*looking out*) There's someone out there keeping an eye on us . . . see him?

POLEVOY (*nervously*) Where?

KETSCHER Let's move.

Stankevich takes a glass of tea.

SAZONOV (*to Ogarev*) We're going, Nick. (*to Stankevich, putting a coin on the table*) Ten absolute kopecks, Stankevich.

POLEVOY We shouldn't stay together.

OGAREV (*to Herzen*) Are you coming, Sasha?

POLEVOY You understand, Herzen. They can ban the *Telegraph* like that—(*He snaps his fingers.*)—and the voice of reform in Russia will be silenced for a generation.

HERZEN To reform this oriental despotism will take more than the oriental tact of the *Telegraph,* Mr Polevoy.

POLEVOY (*stung*) And what are you for, Herzen, you and your circle? Republicanism? Socialism? Anarchism?

HERZEN Yes. We have renounced our right to be the gaolers in a population of prisoners. There's no air, no movement. Words are become deeds. Thoughts are deeds. They're punished more severely than ordinary crimes. We are revolutionaries with secret arsenals of social theory.

POLEVOY What are you reading?

HERZEN Saint-Simon.

POLEVOY A cloak for sensuality and immoral behaviour! . . . God protect our young men and women from Saint-Simon!

HERZEN Why, Mr Polevoy, I do believe you're as old-fashioned a conservative as the people you've been fighting all your life.

Polevoy is deeply offended.

POLEVOY   I see how it is. Well, it will happen to you one day . . . some young man with a smile on his face, telling you, 'Be off with you, you're behind the times!' . . . So, I'll oblige you. My respects, sir . . .

HERZEN (*contrite*)   And mine, Mr Polevoy, believe me

Polevoy hurries away.

HERZEN (*cont.*) (*looking out*)   He's still there . . . Shoulder-first along the tree line like a wolf breaking cover, a starved wolf . . . well, good luck to him, he needs a new coat.

STANKEVICH (*ignoring, looking about*)   Yes . . . you're right . . . something wrong . . . Summer sunshine and the skating ground still frozen, it's a day made up of different days, unaccountable to the diurnal round. (*looking out*) No . . . he's waiting for me. (*to Herzen*) You offended Mr Polevoy for nothing, you know. Political arrangements are merely changing forms in the world of appearances.

HERZEN (*politely*)   I hope you're better soon. (*Looks out.*) Why don't you go and see what he wants? (*He finishes his ice cream and puts money on the table.*) What are we going to do about Russia? I exclude you, Stankevich, but what is to be done? Do you remember Sungurov? When Sungurov was being taken to Siberia, he managed to give his escorting officer the slip . . . but the police got on his track and when he saw there was no escape, he cut his throat but not enough, so they tried him again, and sent him to the mines, and his property was confiscated. This property consisted of two hundred and fifty souls in the Bronnitsky district of Moscow, and four hundred and fifty souls in Nizhny Novgorod. What is wrong with this picture? Nothing. It's Russia. A landowner's estate is reckoned not in acres but in adult male serfs, and the agent of reform is not the rebellious slave but the repentant master.

What a country! Napoleon had to drag us into Europe before our embarrassment at ourselves put seditious thoughts of reform into the heads of the returning army officers. I was thirteen at the time of the December revolt. One day, not long after the Tsar celebrated his coronation by hanging the Decembrists, my father took me and Ogarev for a drive into the country. Until I met Nick I thought I was the only boy like me in the whole of Russia. At Luzhniki we crossed the river. Nick and I ran on ahead, up to the Sparrow Hills. At the top you could see all the roofs and cupolas of the city shining in the setting sun . . . and we suddenly embraced and made a sacred vow to dedicate our lives—yes, sacrifice them if need be—to avenge the Decembrists. It was the hinge of my life.

STANKEVICH   For me it was reading Schelling's *System of Transcendental Idealism*.

HERZEN   That is . . . almost unforgivable.

STANKEVICH   Reform can't come from above or below, only from within. The material world is nothing but the shadow on the wall of the cave. The convulsions of whole societies, in their frantic adjustment of advantage, are the perturbed, deformed spirit objectified on the wall of the cave. (*He raises an arm in farewell.*) Until we meet again.

HERZEN (*coldly*)   But we may *not* meet again.

They separate and Herzen leaves. Belinsky enters. He looks and is almost reduced to beggary, and badly needs a new coat. He is excited.

BELINSKY (*calls out*)   Stankevich! Something good at last. Nadezhdin has offered me work on the *Telescope*. He's going to pay me sixty-four roubles a month.

STANKEVICH   You can't live on that.

BELINSKY I've been living without it.

STANKEVICH Of course you have, look at you, but you can't live *on* it.

BELINSKY But what else can I do?

STANKEVICH Be . . . an artist. Or a philosopher. Everything now depends on artists and philosophers. Great artists to express what can't be explained, philosophers to explain it!

BELINSKY What I *want* to be is a literary critic.

STANKEVICH That's a job for people whose second book didn't come up to expectations. Nadezhdin will have you reviewing twenty books a month for your sixty-four roubles, cookbooks, jokebooks, guidebooks . . .

BELINSKY No, the job is to translate French novels for the *Telescope* . . . I'm translating Paul de Kock . . .

STANKEVICH Oh, you're going to be a *translator*. That's a completely different matter. That is a gentleman's occupation.

BELINSKY You approve.

STANKEVICH But . . . you don't know French.

BELINSKY I know I don't. Can you lend me a dictionary?

They are interrupted by NATALIE BEYER *calling from offstage.*

NATALIE Nicholas! Nicholas!

Stankevich waves to her.

BELINSKY Where will you be later?

STANKEVICH Don't run away—you're clever enough to look Natalie Beyer in the eye, so don't look at her boots.

Natalie, aged twenty, enters from the skating ground, tottering on skates.

NATALIE Nicholas, you're just in time to help me.

She puts one foot up on his thigh and gives him her skate key.

NATALIE (*cont.*) There, *mon chevalier.*

STANKEVICH *A votre service.* Belinsky's got a job on the
Telescope.

NATALIE (*rapidly*) *C'est merveilleux. Vous voulez dire que vous
allez écrire pour la revue? Mais c'est formidable. Nous allons vous
lire. Nous lisons le* Télescope *tous les mois, mais je ne comprends
pas la moitié—vous devez être très intelligent! Vous serez célèbre
sous peu, Monsieur Belinsky!* [How wonderful! Do you mean
to say you'll be writing things in the magazine? But how
exciting. We'll be your readers! We take the Telescope
every month, but I don't understand half the stuff in it—
you must be so clever! You'll be famous in no time, Mr
Belinsky! We'll all be proud to know you.]

Belinsky stares at her boots.

BELINSKY *Au revoir,* then.

STANKEVICH You'll come on Friday?

BELINSKY (*going*) I don't think so . . . I have to do three
chapters by next week.

*Mrs Beyer, Varvara and Liubov return, to meet Natalie. Belinsky,
seeing them coming, hastens his exit.*

MRS BEYER They've got an estate at Voronezh, seven
thousand souls. He's teaching Natalie how everything's
philosophical underneath on Fridays.

VARVARA   Why only on Fridays?

NATALIE   Liubov! Hello, Mrs Bakunin.

MRS BEYER   Take your foot down, whatever next? Mr
Stankevich, how are you? You must come and see us soon.

NATALIE   You'll have to kneel at my feet instead. This is my
friend Liubov Bakunin and her mama.

Stankevich bows.

LIUBOV   Let me do it. Where's the key?

*Stankevich gives Liubov the skate key. The moment of contact
increases Liubov's shyness.*

MRS BEYER   The ice is melting, look . . . The year can get on
now . . .

NATALIE   You must come to the Philosophical Circle,
Liubov. We meet every week in Nicholas's rooms.

STANKEVICH   Do you live in Moscow?

LIUBOV   No.

VARVARA   We're just up for a few days. But we have
philosophy in Tver, too. You must meet my son Michael.

STANKEVICH   Is he studying philosophy?

VARVARA   Yes, he's at the Artillery School.

Liubov comes up with the skates.

LIUBOV   There.

MRS BEYER   We must keep moving. Don't forget, Mr
Stankevich.

Mrs Beyer leaves with Varvara. Stankevich bows the group on its way, then changes his mind.

STANKEVICH I'll come as far as your carriage. (*to Liubov, offering to carry the skates*) Allow me . . .

Liubov gives him the skates.

STANKEVICH (*cont.*) (*to Liubov*) We're reading Schelling at the moment. Perhaps you . . . ?

NATALIE Are you going to carry my skates? How gallant!

Natalie, Liubov and Stankevich follow Varvara and Mrs Beyer out.

The weather changes . . . storm clouds, rain, darkness visible.

Belinsky, with his hunched-over averted gait, is on his way to the Soirée, now wearing a better coat.

MARCH 1835

The Soirée is a regular 'open house' at Mrs Beyer's residence. The presence of liveried servants does not betoken great wealth or opulent surroundings. The livery is more likely to be shabby, and the scale of things is domestic rather than ducal. A Liveried Servant takes Belinsky's dripping coat. The party within is more peripatetic than sedentary. People move into view as occasion requires them. There is more movement and overlap than would be inferred from the sequential description of the scene. Wine, food, Footmen, Guests and music and dancing as may be. Tatiana and Alexandra hurry by, laughing conspiratorially, holding hands.

TATIANA She didn't!

ALEXANDRA She did. But he wouldn't.

They are convulsed with laughter again. PETER CHAADAEV, *aged forty-one, high-domed and bald, a gentleman philosopher, bows to them as they run off with their secret. He establishes himself in a tucked-away chair, more given to receiving an audience than seeking it.*

CHAADAEV   Delightful . . . delightful , , , Young people . . .

Elsewhere STEPAN SHEVYREV, *a young professor, is reading indignantly from a journal (the* Telescope) *to Polevoy, who is slightly drunk and paying little attention.*

SHEVYREV *(reading)*   '. . . I stubbornly hold to the fateful belief'—listen to this—'I stubbornly hold to the fateful belief—'

POLEVOY *(gloomily)*   Closed down. *(He snaps his fingers.)* Like that. I made the *Telegraph* the lone voice of reform.

SHEVYREV   Do you want to hear this?

POLEVOY   Of course, of course. What?

SHEVYREV   This upstart—a *raznochinetz*—a failed student, in fact, picked out of the gutter by Nadezhdin—using the *Telescope* to hold up to ridicule our best, our finest—listen to this—'I stubbornly hold—'

POLEVOY   Nadezhdin should try editing a real magazine. The *Telegraph* played with fire—not my words, words spoken in the Third Section and carried back to me!

SHEVYREV   You don't want me to read it.

POLEVOY   Yes, I do.

SHEVYREV   'I stubbornly—'

POLEVOY But to be closed down—(*He snaps his fingers.*)—like that—*for giving a play a bad notice!*

SHEVYREV 'I stubbornly hold to the fateful belief that despite the fact that our Sumarokov far outstrips Corneille and Racine in tragedy, despite the fact that our Kheraskov has made himself the equal of Homer and Virgil—that our Russian wit Brambeus leaves Voltaire trampled in his dust—'

Ketscher, moderately drunk, enters Polevoy's orbit.

POLEVOY Ketscher! You heard? (*He snaps his fingers.*) The *Telegraph* played with fire once too often!

SHEVYREV '—that our young lion Kukolnik has at his first bound overtaken the genius of Goethe—'

Belinsky enters the party timidly, and, hearing his own words being read aloud, turns tail.

SHEVYREV (*cont.*) '—and at his second, fallen short only of Kryukovsky—despite all this, I say and say again—'

Belinsky, leaving, collides with Michael, who is in military uniform. They don't know each other. Belinsky apologises blindly and leaves.

SHEVYREV (*cont.*) '—we have no literature!'

POLEVOY (*to Ketscher*) I'm lucky not to be in Siberia. And so are you, by the way. Why didn't they arrest you when they arrested Herzen and the others?

KETSCHER (*shrugs*) Russia.

SHEVYREV (*interrupting*) It's not literary criticism, it's iconoclasm for its own sake!

Polevoy draws Ketscher aside as Mrs Beyer and Varvara enter, meeting Michael, who now has Tatiana on his arm.

POLEVOY   I warned them. They destroyed themselves for nothing.

VARVARA   Michael! I don't understand why you aren't with your regiment.

MICHAEL (*leaving*)   My commanding officer keeps asking me the same thing.

VARVARA (*following Michael and Tatiana out*)   Michael . . . !

Shevyrev fastens himself on Varvara, leaving with her.

SHEVYREV   Have you seen the *Telescope*? Listen to this—'I stubbornly hold to the fateful belief . . .'

Mrs Beyer spots Chaadaev and heads for him. Stankevich, entering, bows to her. To his bewilderment Mrs Beyer cuts him.

STANKEVICH   Mrs Beyer.

POLEVOY (*snapping his fingers at Mrs Beyer*)   Like that!

MRS BEYER (*vaguely*)   Mr Polevoy . . . (*to Chaadaev*) Peter!

Stankevich leaves. Chaadaev greets Mrs Beyer.

KETSCHER (*to Polevoy, meanwhile*)   Sentenced in secret after nine months in custody. Three got prison, six got exile, Herzen the furthest—to Perm. All for some loose talk at a supper party Herzen wasn't even at. The joke is, Sazonov, who was there, wasn't even arrested, and now they've given him a passport to go abroad for his health! If these people were doctors, they'd look up your arse for your tonsils . . .

CHAADAEV (*to Mrs Beyer*)   Your house is a haven from, in my case, idleness.

MRS BEYER   I've been telling everybody that you've written that *très méchant* article in the *Telescope*.

CHAADAEV Yes, I saw it . . . It's an interesting moment.

MRS BEYER A moment?

CHAADAEV A moment, yes.

Polevoy, unbidden, includes them in his orbit, deserting Ketscher.

POLEVOY Yes, the *Telegraph* played with fire once too often!

MRS BEYER We're speaking of the *Telescope,* Mr Polevoy.

POLEVOY I beg to correct you, dear lady. I should know—I made the *Telegraph* the voice of reform, I flatter myself I had the ear of His Majesty . . . But who'd have guessed it? Closed down for a bad review of Kukolnik's new play!

CHAADAEV You might have guessed that a play which unites the interests of God and His Majesty's ancestors would have the approval of the Royal Family.

POLEVOY Have you seen it, sir?

CHAADAEV No, I wasn't in St Petersburg.

MRS BEYER You're going to look very silly, Mr Polevoy, aren't you, in a hundred years when *The Hand of the Almighty Saved the Fatherland* is a classic and the name of Kukolnik is synonymous with Russian theatre.

Offstage, a table is knocked over, with a sound of toppling glasses and local alarm and dismay. Belinsky backs into view, apologising and followed by Stankevich. Ketscher hastens grandly to the mishap.

KETSCHER Stand back! I'm a doctor!

MRS BEYER Now what?

BELINSKY I knew it would be like this!

STANKEVICH It's all right, Belinsky . . .

Belinsky tries to flee. Stankevich, trying to hold him back, pulls him by the coat pocket, which rips. A coin or two and a small penknife fall to the floor. Belinsky heedlessly blunders away.

STANKEVICH (*cont.*)   Wait . . . You've dropped your . . .

Stankevich picks up the coins as Mrs Beyer, leaving to investigate, encounters him in what appears to her a posture of supplication. She indicates her impatience and continues out.

POLEVOY (*to Chaadaev*)   But no doubt you have read Kukolnik's play?

CHAADAEV   No . . . I started to read it, but after a while I seemed to lose interest, and I was still on the title.

Stankevich, searching the floor, is interrupted by Natalie entering.

NATALIE   What are you doing?

STANKEVICH   Natalie!—your mother . . . What have I done?

NATALIE   She . . . (*firmly*) Well, Nicholas, you've let her believe you . . . you've been playing with my affections!

POLEVOY (*leaving, snaps his fingers, to no one*)   Like that!

STANKEVICH (*staggered*)   But . . . in all the times I've come to your house, in the whole year you've been coming to our meetings, have I ever by word or gesture sullied the pure spirituality of our—

NATALIE (*losing her temper*)   It's *more* than a year!

She goes out, leaving Stankevich baffled, and returns immediately.

NATALIE (*cont.*) (*changing tack*)   You . . . you have been cruel to my friend Liubov Bakunin!

STANKEVICH   How? I never even . . .

NATALIE   Can't you see she likes you?

STANKEVICH (*with interest*)   Really?

Natalie leaves furiously. Michael, entering, tries to detain her.

MICHAEL   Natalie . . . ?

Michael sees Stankevich. They acknowledge each other with a small bow.

MICHAEL (*cont.*)   Are you Stankevich?

STANKEVICH   You're Bakunin.

Michael shakes Stankevich's hand energetically.

MICHAEL   I thought we were never going to meet.

STANKEVICH   Your sisters . . .

MICHAEL   Have mentioned my existence?

STANKEVICH   In a word. How long are you here?

MICHAEL   A week or so. They're going home tomorrow, but I've got business in Moscow, Army business.

STANKEVICH   You're in the Artillery?

MICHAEL   Don't be deceived by appearances.

STANKEVICH   I'm studying not to be.

MICHAEL   Study is difficult in the Artillery, owing to the loud explosions which are a regular feature of Artillery life. *The System of Transcendental Idealism* is a closed book in the Army, which works on completely different principles.

STANKEVICH   You're reading Schelling!

MICHAEL   Of course! You see before you a single spark from the indivisible fire of creation, a moment in the eternal struggle of Nature towards consciousness.

STANKEVICH But you must read Kant. We are all Kantians, including Schelling.

MICHAEL Thank God I met you. Where can we go and talk? Do you like oysters? Good. Wait here—I'll get my cap, back in a moment. (*turning back*) Have you got any money on you?

STANKEVICH (*obliging*) Yes . . .

MICHAEL Later.

Michael leaves. Stankevich after a moment remembers the lost penknife and vaguely resumes his search.

Alexandra and Tatiana pass through rapidly, intercepted by Natalie, who changes course to exit with them.

NATALIE My friends! I know everything!

SISTERS What? What?

NATALIE His heart beats for another!—wait till I tell you!

SISTERS No! Who? How do you know? I thought he liked you!

NATALIE He led me up the garden!

As they leave, Liubov enters.

SISTERS Liubov! Hello, Liubov! Guess what!

Natalie veers away, pulling Alexandra and Tatiana with her. The three leave, Alexandra and Tatiana questioningly, Natalie whispering to them.

CHAADAEV Delightful, delightful . . .

Stankevich becomes aware of Liubov. He straightens up from his search and bows to her, struck dumb with reserve.

LIUBOV Have you lost something?

STANKEVICH I . . . I'm looking for . . . I think it was a penknife . . . (*Pause.*) So you're going home tomorrow.

LIUBOV Yes. But perhaps . . .

Before Liubov can continue, Stankevich is swept up in Michael's return and departure.

MICHAEL Let's go! Liubov! . . . I've met Stankevich, as you see. We're off to talk about Kant. Kant is the man. Oh, the time I've wasted! From now on . . .

LIUBOV *Michael* . . .

MICHAEL What?

LIUBOV (*improvising*) What about . . . the Army?

MICHAEL Don't worry, I've got it in hand. (*as they go*) You must come and stay with us at Premukhino. Will you come?

He sweeps Stankevich out, almost colliding with Belinsky.

LIUBOV Premukhino . . . !

Belinsky notices her. He knows her. Liubov is unaware of him. As she turns to leave, she sees the penknife on the floor. She gives a little cry of joy and picks it up.

BELINSKY Oh . . . I think that's my . . .

Liubov presses the penknife to her lips and puts it in her neckline. She sees Belinsky.

LIUBOV Oh . . .

Belinsky, stupefied, bows to her.

BELINSKY I am deeply . . . deeply . . .

LIUBOV Forgive me . . . I'm so . . .

BELINSKY Don't be! I am deeply . . . deeply . . .

LIUBOV I've got such an awful memory, you see.

BELINSKY Memory? Oh. (*adjusting*) Belinsky. Philosophy Circle. Friday.

LIUBOV Yes. That's where it was. I'm so sorry. Goodbye, Mr Belinsky. We're going home tomorrow.

Liubov leaves.

Shevyrev enters, intent on Chaadaev.

BELINSKY (*to himself*) Fool!

Shevyrev hesitates, surprised. Belinsky recovers.

BELINSKY (*cont.*) Professor Shevyrev!—It's Belinsky. I was in your History of Russian Literature class.

SHEVYREV That's impossible. We have no literature.

Snubbed, Belinsky retreats as Shevyrev obsequiously approaches Chaadaev.

SHEVYREV (*cont.*) I believe I have the honour of addressing Peter Chaadaev. May I offer my admiration for your book . . .

CHAADAEV My book?

SHEVYREV *The Philosophical Letters . . .*

CHAADAEV Ah. Thank you. I was not aware that it had been published.

SHEVYREV That has not prevented it from attracting a host of admirers . . . few, I daresay, as enthusiastic as—(*He bows.*)—

Stepan Shevyrev, Professor of the History of Literature at Moscow University. (*He takes a sheaf of manuscript pages from his pocket.*) My copy of the first Letter, sir—a late and undistinguished progeny of the archetype.

CHAADAEV May I see? (*He glances at it.*) Not even that. I wrote in French. I wrote, as it happens, that we Russians, belonging neither to East nor West, have never advanced with other people in the march of enlightenment. The Renaissance passed us by while we remained squatting in our hovels . . . And here are my words, copied, translated, and copied again . . . as though bearing witness to an age before the printing press.

SHEVYREV Yes, a difficult book from the point of view of publication. It is in that regard that I make myself known to you. A group of us at the University have been granted a licence to publish a new literary journal which will be called the *Moscow Observer* . . . and it would give us great pleasure to bring *The Philosophical Letters* to the reading public. (*Pause.*) If you would do us the honour. (*Pause.*) Subject, of course, to getting it through the censor. (*Pause.*) Which I believe we can do by altering a word or two. (*Pause.*) Two, in fact. I would ask your permission to alter two words. (*Pause.*) 'Russia' . . . and . . . 'We.'

CHAADAEV 'Russia' and 'We'.

SHEVYREV 'We,' 'us,' 'our' . . . they're like warning flags to the Censor.

CHAADAEV And in their place . . . what . . . ?

SHEVYREV I would suggest 'Certain people.'

CHAADAEV 'Certain people.'

SHEVYREV Yes.

CHAADAEV Ingenious.

SHEVYREV Thank you.

CHAADAEV (*experimentally*) 'Certain people, belonging neither to East nor West, have never advanced with other people . . . The Renaissance passed certain people by . . . certain people remained squatting in certain people's hovels . . .' (*He returns the pages.*) . . . Would you allow me to think it over?

Shevyrev bows himself away.

Alexandra and Tatiana hurry by in agitated conference.

TATIANA Poor Natalie.

ALEXANDRA She gave him up for love!

They hurry out.

CHAADAEV Delightful . . . delightful . . .

In the transition, Liubov dances privately across the stage and, just before leaving, suddenly twirls out of sight.

MARCH 1835

The transition is to daylight, a week later. Natalie runs into the room, slightly hysterical. Michael follows, slightly sheepish.

NATALIE It must be *my* fault. Otherwise how could it be that *both* of you . . . It's so humiliating!

MICHAEL Yes, but Nicholas and I humiliated you in different ways, don't forget that.

NATALIE I don't care about him anymore.

MICHAEL With Nicholas it's self-control.

NATALIE (*incredulously*) He was controlling himself?

MICHAEL Well, probably not in your case . . .

NATALIE (*flaring*) What do you mean?

MICHAEL Yours was just a misunderstanding, but last year the young wife of one of his neighbours in the country took him into their summerhouse and kissed him and pulled down her whatever it was, and—

NATALIE You've only known him a week!

MICHAEL He told me a week ago, we were discussing transcendental idealism over oysters, and one thing led to another.

NATALIE Yes, I see. Well, what happened?

MICHAEL Well—we got on to the separation of spirit and matter—

NATALIE In the summerhouse.

MICHAEL Well, she asked him to kiss her—her—her—you know . . .

NATALIE She didn't!

MICHAEL She did. *Both* her . . . both of them.

NATALIE Oh. Go on, anyway.

MICHAEL I've just remembered something.

NATALIE What?

MICHAEL I promised not to tell anyone.

NATALIE   You can't stop *now*!

MICHAEL   No, I really shouldn't—

NATALIE   *Michael!*

MICHAEL   (*hastily*)   Well, he was kissing her dugs when he
suddenly realised that what he'd *thought* was his soul
reaching out for communion with hers, was *actually* a
negation of the transcendence of spirit over matter . . . and
he couldn't go on, he was repelled . . . nauseated . . .

NATALIE   He explained this to her, did he?

MICHAEL   No, he ran away. That's the difference between
Stankevich and me.

NATALIE   What is?

MICHAEL   I'm put off before I begin. Not by you, not by you.

NATALIE   I don't understand why it's called romanticism.
(*bewildered*) It's all so different in George Sand.

MICHAEL   I think you're the one who can give me faith in
myself, Natalie. Schelling doesn't understand the point of
his own philosophy, if you ask me. Transcending to the
Universal Idea means to put a bomb under our submission
to habit and convention—in short, to give oneself utterly to
loving humanity, to love our neighbour and our
neighbour's wife—to release the passion of our nature—

NATALIE   Yes! And you *will*, because I understand you as no
one else, not even your sisters.

MICHAEL   My sisters?

NATALIE   They love you, but do they *see* you?—your inner
reality?

MICHAEL Perhaps not . . .

NATALIE They haven't transcended the objective reality in which you're just their brother.

MICHAEL (*enlightened*) Well—no wonder!

NATALIE I can explain it to them. I'll give you a letter for them to read when you go home.

MICHAEL Yes, that should do the trick.

SUMMER 1835

The Telescope *office is sufficient for the editing of a small-circulation literary magazine, and is as much an ordinary room as it is an office. There is an entrance door and a door to an inner room.*

Chaadaev sits waiting. Belinsky enters from within with galleys and page proofs and goes to the only desk. Chaadaev stands up. Belinsky is surprised to see him. He has no more social ease than before.

CHAADAEV Chaadaev.

BELINSKY Belinsky.

CHAADAEV Is Professor Nadezhdin . . . ?

BELINSKY Not yet, no. I'm expecting him back anytime.

CHAADAEV Ah. May I sit down?

BELINSKY Yes. There's a chair.

Chaadaev sits. Pause. Belinsky stands waiting.

CHAADAEV Please don't let me stop you from . . .

BELINSKY (*nonplussed*) Oh. Thank you.

Belinsky sits at the desk but is fidgety. Time passes.

CHAADAEV Is Nadezhdin at lunch?

BELINSKY No, he's in the Caucasus.

CHAADAEV Ah. Well . . . in that case . . .

BELINSKY I'm expecting him back any day.

CHAADAEV Even so.

BELINSKY (*flustered*) I didn't quite understand . . .

CHAADAEV My fault entirely.

BELINSKY He went to the Caucasus for a few months.

CHAADAEV Of course.

BELINSKY He left me in charge.

CHAADAEV Really? If I may say so, there has been a noticeable improvement in the quality of the *Telescope* which has more than made up for the irregularity of its appearance.

BELINSKY (*gloomily*) Ah, you noticed that.

CHAADAEV Don't worry. If only Shevyrev had the wit to miss out on a few issues of the *Observer*, where one would be grateful for the respite.

Belinsky cheers up instantly, becoming almost gleeful, losing his shyness. On home ground—literature and criticism—he becomes transformed.

BELINSKY Yes! I'm preparing an article against him. There'll be no mercy for Shevyrev! I thought I was going to be literally sick when I read his essay on the genteel. Gentility and art are not synonyms. Gentility is the property of caste. Art is the property of intelligence and feeling. Otherwise, any toff could walk in here and call himself a writer.

CHAADAEV (*politely*) Quite . . .

BELINSKY I'm losing my youth and my health and making enemies all over the shop when I could be surrounded by admirers who want nothing from me except to take away my independence—because I believe literature alone can, even now, redeem our honour, even now, in words alone, that have ducked and dodged their way past the censor, literature can be . . . become . . . can . . . (*furiously*) I don't know what I'm saying half the time, but that's the half that's as plain to me as a glass of water!

CHAADAEV You mean literature can make itself useful, with a social purpose . . . ?

BELINSKY No! Let social purpose hang itself unhindered! No—I mean, literature can *replace,* can actually *become* . . . Russia! It can be greater and more real than the external reality. It only has to be true. Art is true or false. Everything else about it is up to the artist, but on *that* we're in the emperor's seat. (*He puts his thumb up, then down.*) Hail or good night. Not true to the *facts,* not true to appearances, but true to the innermost of the innermost doll, where genius and nature are the same stuff. The moment an artist has a thesis, he is merely a huckster, maybe talented but that's not it, it won't help us when every time we say 'Russia' we have to grin and twitch like half-wits from the embarrassment of a mother country that has given nothing to the world and taken nothing from it. 'Russia! Yes, I'm afraid so—you've got it—the backwoods—no history but barbarism, no law but autocracy, no glory but brute force, and all those contented serfs!'—we're nothing to the world except an object lesson in what to avoid. But a great artist can change all that, make it irrelevant, well, not one, but even one, even Pushkin for a start, I mean Pushkin up to,

say, *Boris Gudunov,* he's finished now, he hasn't written a
great poem for years, but even Pushkin, or Gogol's new
stories, definitely Gogol, and there's more to come, I know
they're coming, and soon, here things are growing not by
the year but by the *hour,* every time I open a new
manuscript I wonder whether it's going to make last week's
Telescope completely out of date. You see what I'm saying?
When the word 'Russia' makes you think of great writers
and almost nothing else, the job will be done—you'll be able
to walk down the street in London or Paris, and when
someone asks you where you're from, you can say, 'Russia!
I'm from Russia, you poor bastard, so what do you think of
that?!'

CHAADAEV (*Pause.*)   It's actually not too late to amend last
week's *Telescope.*

BELINSKY   Oh God, I know! I'm still writing some of it.

CHAADAEV   If I may speak to you as an admirer, it is not your
beliefs which make you enemies, so much as your . . . your
style . . . People aren't used to it.

BELINSKY   But what can I do? When a book seizes me, it's
not by the elbow but by the throat. I have to slap down
my thoughts before I lose them, and change them
sometimes while I'm having them—it all goes in, there's
no time to have a style, it's a miracle if I have a main verb.
What people are *used* to is deference to literature's own
table of ranks. We've always awarded laurels too easily, but
at least in the old days it was out of childish veneration.
Now it's a gang of St Petersburg toadies rigging
reputations like stocks they've got shares in. Bulgarin,
Grech and Senkowski can have their style. Mine is chaos,
excess and no mercy.

CHAADAEV Yes . . . an interesting moment. (*preparing to go, hesitates*) I happen to know Pushkin. If you like, I'll give him your good wishes.

BELINSKY For his recovery. Oh, bite your tongue, Belinsky! Yes—give Mr Pushkin my . . . adoration. Ask him to give me a poem, so I have something for Nadezhdin.

CHAADAEV (*deciding*) I have brought something of mine for Nadezhdin. Here. It's not new. Perhaps you already know it.

He gives a manuscript to Belinsky, who studies it for a moment.

BELINSKY No . . .

CHAADAEV It's probably unpublishable.

BELINSKY Oh, I'm sure it's not that bad.

CHAADAEV In Russia, that is.

BELINSKY Ah, yes.

CHAADAEV I share your sentiments, even one or two of your phrases . . . (*taking the pages*) Allow me . . . here, for instance: '. . . *nous sommes du nombre de ces nations qui ne semblent pas faire partie intégrante du genre humain, n'est qui existe que pour donner leçon au monde* . . .'

BELINSKY (*faking*) Ah. Yes . . . indeed . . . indeed . . .

CHAADAEV And this paragraph especially. I am not an artist, so I trust you will allow me to have a thesis. How did we come to be the Caliban of Europe? We stand with one foot in the air, do we not, needing to repeat the whole education of man, which passed us by.

BELINSKY (*faking*) Oh . . . yes . . . yes . . .

Chaadaev is disappointed and puzzled by Belinsky's deflated response.

CHAADAEV Well—(*preparing to leave again*)—no doubt
Nadezhdin will tell me if he's willing to tussle with
the censor. I hope it's not too . . . genteel for your
taste.

BELINSKY (*looking at the pages*) No . . . no . . .

*His little joke having failed to register, Chaadaev, slightly on the
wrong foot, leaves. As soon as he is safely gone, Belinsky hurls
himself into a fury of humiliated self-castigation, assaulting himself,
hitting the furniture and finally rolling on the floor. Chaadaev re-
enters, catching him.*

CHAADAEV My fault entirely. I'll send you a copy in Russian.

He bows and leaves.
Belinsky sits in the desk chair and buries his face in his arms.

SPRING 1836

*Belinsky is asleep at his desk with his head in his arms. He wakes
when Michael enters.*

MICHAEL Belinsky . . .

BELINSKY Oh . . . Bakunin . . . sorry . . . Come in! Please.
Have a chair. What time is it?

MICHAEL I don't know. Is Nadezhdin here?

BELINSKY No. He's arguing over an article at the censor's
office.

MICHAEL Damn . . . Never mind, listen, how much money
do you have on you?

BELINSKY Me? I'm sorry, I wish I . . .

MICHAEL   I'm not trying to borrow it.

BELINSKY   Oh, well, I've got about fifteen roubles.

MICHAEL   That will have to do for the moment. It's for this
article I've done for the *Telescope*. (*He gives Belinsky a few
sheets.*) It's a pity you weren't at the last meeting.
Stankevich and I have discovered a new philosophy.

BELINSKY   I *was* there. Could you wait till Nadezhdin gets
back? . . . Oh, it's a translation . . . Fichte.

MICHAEL   Stankevich went through it with me before he left.
He's taken his cough to the Caucasus. It sounds as if you
should do the same. What do you think?

BELINSKY   How can I . . . ?

MICHAEL   Yes, you're right, you have to read it first. Fichte is
the man! Now I know why nothing ever seemed quite right.
Schelling was trying to make out I was just some insignificant
spark of consciousness in the Great Pre-Conscious, but the
Self won't be got rid of like that. How do I know I exist?
Not by meditation! In meditation I *cease* to exist. I know I
exist when a seagull shits on my head. The world achieves
existence where I meet it. (*He demonstrates with a stale bread roll
snatched from the desk.*) I don't eat because it's food, it's food
because I eat it. Because I decide it. Because I will it. The
world is nothing but the impress of my Self. The Self is
everything, it's the *only* thing. At last a philosophy that makes
sense! You can read it while I've got a letter to write, don't
move, I'll use Nadezhdin's desk.

BELINSKY   No, you can't go in, he's got someone waiting—

MICHAEL   I say, Belinsky, what do you know about Sollogub?
I'm told he writes.

BELINSKY He's a fop. Stories about high society, not contemptible, though worthless.

MICHAEL Good-looking? Good horseman, good shot, one of those? Well, I'll see him off anyway. It seems he's pursuing poor Tatiana— Natalie's had a letter from my sisters . . . Oh, I forgot— (He opens the door and bawls.) Porter! Ask Miss Beyer to come up! . . . By the way—(He gives Belinsky a few visiting cards.)—did I show you these? 'Monsieur de Bacounine . . . *Maître de Mathématiques* . . .'

BELINSKY Yes, you gave me one. Did you get any pupils?

MICHAEL One step at a time. If you hear of anyone . . . My father let me down, let me down very badly, trying to shove me into the Governor's office in Tver, it served him right when I washed my hands of home sweet home . . . but God, I miss it sometimes, and now Stankevich has left town and the Beyers are leaving for the country soon . . . I'm thinking of forgiving him. Why don't you come and stay?

BELINSKY Come . . . ?

MICHAEL To Premukhino. We can study Fichte together.

BELINSKY Oh, I'd only make a fool of myself there.

MICHAEL It's not grand, all you need is a clean shirt . . . perhaps a pair of shoes . . . I'd give you the money right now, only just at this moment . . . That's why I'm obliged to ask you for cash on the nail—it's the last thing I'll ever ask of you.

BELINSKY I can't give it to you, I'm sorry, I'm . . . meeting someone later.

MICHAEL (*without resentment*) Another tart up from the country?

BELINSKY   No, the same one.

Natalie enters behind him.

BELINSKY (*cont.*)   At least she's a real woman, even if she's a tart.

MICHAEL (*to Natalie*)   He's not talking about you.

NATALIE (*resigned*)   I know.

MICHAEL   I'm going to write to Tatiana while I'm here.

BELINSKY   Miss Beyer . . .

NATALIE   Hello, Vissarion. You didn't come to the Philosophy Circle.

BELINSKY   Yes, I did.

Michael meanwhile has half entered the inner room, and returned.

MICHAEL   There's someone asleep in there.

BELINSKY (*fussed*)   I told you . . .

MICHAEL   Who is it?

BELINSKY   Strogonov. A publisher.

MICHAEL   Well, I won't disturb him.

Michael goes inside and closes the door.

BELINSKY   Do you want to sit down?

NATALIE   Thank you. (*She sits.*) Now the chair exists. And I exist where I meet the chair. The real woman you were talking about must spend her life sitting down. Is she a writer?

BELINSKY   Fichte didn't really mean . . . It's the impress of the *mind* upon the world . . . the Self.

NATALIE   At least Fichte makes us all equal, not like in Schelling, where you had to be an artist or a philosopher, a *genius,* to be a moral example to the rest of us.

BELINSKY   Yes! That's right! Democracy in the moral order. Fichte puts us back in the saddle!

NATALIE   So Michael's got no right to be moralistic about Tatiana and Count Sollogub.

BELINSKY   What?

NATALIE   Isn't she allowed to have a saddle?

BELINSKY   Oh . . . ! (*disbelieving*) Tatiana?!

NATALIE   Her sisters wrote me all about it, so I told Michael.

BELINSKY   Is it all right to tell me?

NATALIE   What?

BELINSKY   I don't know.

NATALIE   About letting Count Sollogub write to her?

BELINSKY   What?

NATALIE   Why should Tatiana send the Count's letters back? It's a woman's purpose to be worshipped. A Russian woman, anyway. Or a German woman, of course . . . to be the incarnation of the Ideal, to be a sister, an angel, a Beautiful Soul . . .

Belinsky is distracted by a sound of conversation from the inner room.

NATALIE (*cont.*)   In the perfect society, all women will be the object of exalted feelings, like in the time of the troubadours . . . loved by the pure flame of spiritual . . . (*abruptly*) Was it George Sand?

The sound next door becomes more lively and convivial. Michael laughs.

BELINSKY   I wonder what's going on.

NATALIE (*with sudden passion and anger*)   How dare you call her a tart? George Sand has freed herself from the slavery of our sex!—she's a saint!

BELINSKY (*baffled, alarmed*)   It's all right . . .

NATALIE (*bursts into tears*)   I want to be a French woman. Or Spanish or Italian . . . even Norwegian . . . *Dutch!* . . . or any . . .

Michael comes out of the other room with a book in his hand.

MICHAEL (*gaily*)   Done it!

He gives Natalie his letter, and money to Belinsky. Natalie reads the letter.

BELINSKY   What's this?

MICHAEL   Stroganov's asked me to translate this German history book—eight hundred roubles, half up-front, piece of cake, that'll show them! There you are, get yourself a new pair of shoes, now you've got to come. Off we go, Natalie, my rod, my staff, my disciple, my sister in joy and sorrow—

NATALIE   It's the letter of a jealous lover! You've never written like that to me!

She flings it at him and leaves. Michael picks it up.

MICHAEL   I'll see you at Premukhino.

He follows Natalie out.

INTER-SCENE: NOVEMBER 1836

A piano. Stankevich plays a duet with Liubov. He breaks off and stands up abruptly.

STANKEVICH Liubov! I must speak! While you were away, . . . I have been in . . .

LIUBOV (*helping*) The Caucasus.

STANKEVICH . . . torment! You are not the first. I come to you . . . soiled.

LIUBOV You mustn't speak of it.

STANKEVICH Yes, I must, I must—it lies so heavy on my breast that my lips have touched another's!

LIUBOV (*confused*) Breast?

STANKEVICH (*startled*) Lips, another's lips. (*shrewdly*) Has Michael been telling you . . . ?

LIUBOV No! In you I have found the answering echo of my inner life!

STANKEVICH Am I forgiven?

LIUBOV I don't come to you without a mark, Nicholas.

STANKEVICH Oh, my dear . . .

LIUBOV But compared to our exalted love, what is a kiss in a summerhouse?

STANKEVICH (*jumps*) He *has* told you! Oh, my God!

LIUBOV No!

STANKEVICH Who, then? . . . The priest!

LIUBOV No! No!

STANKEVICH   What are you telling me?

LIUBOV   Baron Renne kissed me in the summerhouse!

STANKEVICH   Oh! I kissed someone in a summerhouse, too. But I didn't like it.

LIUBOV   I didn't like it either. It was just two kisses, Nicholas.

STANKEVICH   (*Pause.*)   Where?

LIUBOV   In the summerhouse.

Pause. They seem about to kiss. He loses courage, sits, and plays again.

DECEMBER 1836

Belinsky's room is a very small space with one window. The larger space suggests the next-door laundry with its steam, its tubs, mangles and washing hung to dry. There is a background of noise from the laundry—the thump of washtubs, water sluicing . . . His room contains a small bed, a stand-up writing desk, a poor couch occupied by books and bundles, and a wood-burning stove. There are journals, magazines, papers piled on the floor, and a basic washstand and chamber pot. A young woman, KATYA, is in bed wearing her clothes, including an overcoat. Belinsky is heard coming up the stairs. He enters carrying pieces of scavenged wood for the stove. He is not expecting to see Katya, who has sat up, afraid until she sees him.

BELINSKY   Katya . . . I thought you'd gone for good. I was worried.

KATYA   Oh, I had such a fright, the police came and searched.

BELINSKY   I know.

KATYA   I was afraid they'd come back.

Belinsky puts the wood by the stove.

BELINSKY   I'll light it when it's colder.

KATYA   They even looked inside the stove.

BELINSKY   Were they correct with you? Did they insult you?

KATYA   Insult me?

BELINSKY   (*drops it*)   Well, if you didn't notice . . . They had me in for questioning. It's lucky I was away in the country all that time. Nadezhdin got exile. (*Laughs.*) The censor has lost his three thousand roubles a year—they say he passed Chaadaev's article in the middle of a card game.

KATYA   You stayed away much longer than you said . . . Why didn't you write to tell me?

BELINSKY   You can't read.

KATYA   That's no reason.

BELINSKY   Yes, I'm sorry. What did you do when the money was gone?

KATYA   Sold my jewels.

BELINSKY   Oh, I hope not, I hope not! (*He embraces her, feeling her body inside her clothes.*) No, they're still there. (*He kisses her.*)

KATYA   What was it like where you went?

BELINSKY   It was . . . a family. Amazing. I knew there were families. I come from a family. But I had no idea.

KATYA   Did you bring me something?

BELINSKY   And the place itself, Premukhino in the freshness
of the early morning, everything chirping and croaking,
whistling, and splashing, as if Nature was having a
conversation with itself, and the sunsets breathing, as alive as
fire . . . You understood how the Eternal and Universal are
more real than your everyday life, than this room and the
world lying in wait outside the room, you believed in the
possibility of escape, of transcendence, of raising your soul
to the necessary height, and living high above your own
life, folded into the mind of the Absolute.

KATYA   (*impatient with him*)   Tell me what happened properly.

BELINSKY   It was awful.

*He gives way, starts to sob. Katya holds him, upset and anxious,
until he recovers.*

KATYA   It's all right . . . it's all right . . . What is it?

BELINSKY   (*recovered*)   Don't you bother with reading, Katya,
words just lead you on. They arrange themselves every
which way, with no can to carry for the promises they can't
keep, and off you go! 'The objective world is the still
unconscious poetry of the soul.' What do these words
mean? 'The spiritual communion of beautiful souls attaining
harmony with the Absolute.' What do they mean?

KATYA   I don't know.

BELINSKY   Nothing, and I understood them perfectly!—my
everyday life, which was banal, meaningless, degrading, was
merely illusion . . . In my real life, my inner life, there was
no cause for misery and humiliation. But when it turned
out the necessary height was a metre or two above my
reach, and all those fine phrases burst like bubbles, there was
nowhere to go except back home feeling worthless and now
without even a job . . .

Michael is heard stamping up the stairs and shouting 'Belinsky!' in an aggressive tone. Katya, without alarm or instruction, pulls the blankets around her, making no real attempt to hide, though becoming almost invisible but for her face. Michael barges in flourishing a letter.

MICHAEL So—do you want to have this out?

BELINSKY Why don't you sit down?

MICHAEL Because there's nowhere to sit and I'm not staying.

BELINSKY You didn't care for my letter.

MICHAEL What I don't care for is being talked down to on a subject you'd know nothing about if Stankevich and I hadn't *translated* it for you and made a *pupil* of you. What I don't care for is being preached at about my character as if I were a ledger clerk, by a snivelling penny-a-line book reviewer who makes himself at home under my roof, insults my parents and makes sheep's eyes at my sister, who could take her pick from the nobility of the province.

Belinsky quails as from a physical assault.

BELINSKY Oh . . . oh . . . so that was it—

MICHAEL Ha!—do you think I care if you make a donkey of yourself over Alexandra? What I object to—what I find disgusting—is that poor Tatiana should be taken in by your mountebank's intellectual posturing and hang on your lips and gaze at you like a . . . like a—

Michael collapses around Belinsky's shoulders weeping.

BELINSKY (*bewildered*) What . . . ? What's the matter?

MICHAEL Tatiana! Tatiana! Forgive me, Belinsky, forgive me, my sins are ten times yours! I don't know what to call my feeling for her—but it ruined me, all my ideals were powerless against my . . . my . . . my jealousy . . .

BELINSKY *You* were jealous of *me*?

MICHAEL I was in torment . . .

Belinsky is moved. He embraces Michael.

BELINSKY Michael, Michael . . .

Michael notices Katya staring at him.

MICHAEL Oh . . . excuse me, madame . . . (*He disengages himself from Belinsky.*) Bakunin. (*to Belinsky*) I really must be going. Stankevich sends his regards. Did I tell you he and Liubov have agreed to correspond? It's a secret, as yet—but their letters are beautiful. I read (*present tense*) them to Natalie and we agree he's worthy of her. Varenka has weakened, I'm afraid—I've had to write to her about that animal Dyakov, but I've got it in hand. I'm sorry if I got a bit . . . you know . . . but we're all right again, aren't we? What will you do without the *Telescope*?

BELINSKY I don't know.

MICHAEL (*cheerfully*) Still, you're lucky not to be in Siberia. Chaadaev's under house arrest. He's officially insane, only nobody's telling him, and His Majesty wants daily reports . . . Well, *à bientôt,* see you on Friday. What are you reading?

BELINSKY Fichte, of course. Why?

MICHAEL You must read Hegel. Hegel is the man! Fichte tried to argue the objective world out of existence. No wonder I was going wrong! . . . (*Bows to Katya.*) Madame, a thousand pardons.

Michael leaves.

KATYA   Huh . . . ! (*Mocks him.*) Alexandra!

Belinsky takes the little penknife from his pocket.

BELINSKY   Here. It's what I brought back for you.

KATYA (*pleased*)   I've never had a penknife.

BELINSKY   It's all I've got left.

INTER-SCENE—JANUARY 1837

Music. Leaning in the doorway of a concert hall, the poet
ALEXANDER PUSHKIN, *aged thirty-seven, scans the audience
with an expression of superior discontent. He catches somebody's eye,
turns away abruptly and leaves.*

There is the sound of an other-worldly distant pistol shot.

FEBRUARY 1837

*Night. Belinsky's room is lit by a tallow lamp. Belinsky, wearing his
coat, is wrapping layers of newsprint across his midriff for extra
warmth, and coughing into a dirty handkerchief. Stankevich, dressed
for outdoors, is pacing, excited, holding open a book.*

STANKEVICH   The first thing we have to do is stop being
Hamlets.

BELINSKY (*reading from his stomach*)   Listen to this—'the death
of the greatest poet who ever lived . . .' God, how I hate
the people who write in the shirtfronts. What's it got to do
with them?—The loss is personal, I refuse to share it.

STANKEVICH His moral and spiritual despair is what comes from refusing to face up to the rationality of the objective world . . .

BELINSKY It was she who killed him, in a way . . .

STANKEVICH That's what I think! She was the wrong woman for him. The duel was between knowledge and denial, the dialectic dramatised, it's all there in Hegel.

BELINSKY Hegel? She was a flirt!

STANKEVICH Well, I have to agree. But on a higher, Hegelian level, duelling with rapiers represents—

BELINSKY He was shot.

STANKEVICH What?

BELINSKY He was shot.

STANKEVICH Who was?

BELINSKY Pushkin.

STANKEVICH I'm talking about Hamlet.

BELINSKY Hamlet?

STANKEVICH Yes, Hamlet. The play was called *Hamlet* by William Shakespeare. There was a duel. Do you remember the duel?

BELINSKY Look, Stankevich, this is humiliating, but whether the objective world is as insubstantial as a fairy's fart or as real as a veal chop—(*He clutches his stomach.*)—oh, don't!—until someone has the sense to offer me the editorship of some . . .

STANKEVICH (*taking an envelope of money from his pocket*) Oh!—that's what I came for. You should go to the Caucasus for a

96

few months. Here. It's not just from me. Botkin, Aksakov, Katkov . . . all the members of the circle . . .

BELINSKY Thank you.

STANKEVICH You have to get yourself . . .

BELINSKY I will. Don't worry.

STANKEVICH You can take Hegel with you.

BELINSKY So, the objective world is not an illusion?

STANKEVICH No.

BELINSKY The laundry, the blacksmith, everything that Fichte said was just the shapes left by the impress of my mind . . . is real?

STANKEVICH Yes. Everything rational is real, and everything real is rational.

BELINSKY Poverty, injustice, censorship, whips and scorns, the law's delay? The Minister for Public Instruction? Russia?

STANKEVICH Real.

BELINSKY How did we miss it?

STANKEVICH Not just real but necessary.

BELINSKY Why's that?

STANKEVICH Necessary to the march of history. The dialectical logic of history.

BELINSKY Really? So, to . . . worry about it . . . deplore it . . . is . . .

STANKEVICH Unintelligent. A vulgar error.

BELINSKY   Can you lend me a dictionary?

STANKEVICH   God knows when I'll see you again. The doctors say I have to take the water cure at Carlsbad. I'm going home to see my parents first.

BELINSKY   Are you to be congratulated yet?

STANKEVICH   No. Not officially. (*Pause.*) Belinsky . . . tell Liubov she's too good for me!

BELINSKY   Have you never felt . . . desire?

STANKEVICH   There was a woman once before . . . (*He abandons the train of thought.*) But I know I experienced a powerful feeling when she was kneeling at my feet . . .

BELINSKY (*sagely*)   In the summerhouse.

STANKEVICH   . . . to take off Natalie's skate . . .

BELINSKY (*too late*)   Skate.

STANKEVICH   Summerhouse?

BELINSKY   What?

STANKEVICH   You said summerhouse.

BELINSKY   Look . . .

STANKEVICH   Bakunin!

BELINSKY   Oh God . . .

STANKEVICH   Bakunin!

In tears of humiliation, Stankevich bolts from the room and falls down the unseen stairs. Belinsky grabs the lamp and follows, cursing himself.

MARCH 1838

Belinsky's room. Michael has moved in with Belinsky. The books and jumble previously on the couch are on the floor. Michael is lying on the couch, smoking and writing. Belinsky, wearing a coat from the Caucasus, is writing feverishly at the stand-up desk, throwing completed pages to join others on the floor. The laundry sounds today are augmented by hammering on an anvil down below. Michael jumps up, opens the window to shout. The laundry sounds and the hammering are louder, and a few soap bubbles enter through the window.

MICHAEL (*shouts*)   Hammer quietly, damn you! (*He closes the window and paces energetically.*) We'll change the cover from yellow to green, so the readers can see straightaway that the *Moscow Observer* is under new management.

Incensed by renewed hammering, he flings himself out of the door and down the stairs, shouting abuse.

Belinsky stops writing to take off his coat. He picks the pages off the floor.

APRIL 1838

There is a transition to another day, a month later. The anvil is silent. The laundry noises are quieter. Belinsky is excited and pleased. He has the green-covered Moscow Observer, *turning the pages. Michael enters and goes straight to his couch, where he starts stuffing his belongings into a big satchel.*

BELINSKY   We should have put April on the cover instead of March . . . There's too much Hegel, perhaps. But your very first signed article reads well . . . (*He notices what Michael is doing.*)

MICHAEL   I've got to go home.

BELINSKY Has something happened?

MICHAEL Agriculture!

BELINSKY What do you mean, agriculture?

MICHAEL That's what *I* said! Stankevich has been in Berlin for months, sitting at the feet of the Professor there, who was Hegel's actual pupil—and my father says he'll pay my debts if I agree to study agriculture!

BELINSKY Why agriculture?

MICHAEL Apparently Premukhino is an agricultural *business.* You thought it was just *there,* didn't you, an aesthetic fact of nature, like a bluebell only much bigger.

BELINSKY No, I didn't.

MICHAEL Well, I did. I had no idea it was *agriculture.* The peasants plant things as their fathers did, the things grow, you eat them or feed the animals with them, and then it's time to plant some more. Country life! It isn't a *subject* for an educated man! So I have to go home and explain things to my father. Anyway, I want to see Varenka before she leaves—and Liubov is worse, I'll cheer her up . . .

BELINSKY Is there any news from Stankevich?

MICHAEL (*gloomily*) He's having second thoughts.

BELINSKY Oh. Has he told her?

MICHAEL No, not about Liubov.

BELINSKY Oh.

MICHAEL He doesn't feel he can ask his father for more money. Honestly!—you should see their estate—*thousands* of souls! I could study Idealism in Berlin for three years for the price of a couple of house serfs! (*Michael has got himself packed and ready to leave.*) In case you're wondering about the *Observer,* I've decided this having-our-own-journal is a mistake.

BELINSKY   A mistake?

MICHAEL   We have to abandon the whole thing. We're not ready.

BELINSKY   For what?

MICHAEL   We have to think—think—think!

BELINSKY   Is this because I made a few cuts in your article . . . ?

MICHAEL   Look, it's simple. We haven't got the right to publish without a lot more study.

BELINSKY   I see.

MICHAEL   Good. That's settled, then. I'm off. (*He embraces Belinsky.*) You're still my Vissarion!

BELINSKY   I've always admired your qualities, your undoubted qualities . . . your energy, optimism . . . The last few months, studying Hegel together and bringing out the first issue of the magazine, have been the happiest of my life. Never have you shown more of the love in you, the gaiety, the poetry. That's how I want to remember you.

MICHAEL   Thank you, Vissarion.

BELINSKY   I don't want to remember you for your overbearing vanity, your selfishness, your lack of scruple . . . your bullying, your cadging, your conceit as teacher and guide to your distracted sisters whose only philosophy is 'Michael says' . . .

MICHAEL   Well!

BELINSKY   . . . and above all your permanent flight into abstraction and fantasy which allows you not to notice that the life of the philosopher is an aristocratic affair made possible by the sweat of Premukhino's five hundred souls who somehow haven't managed to attain oneness with the Absolute.

MICHAEL   Right. I don't remember you saying any of this when you had your snout in the trough.

BELINSKY   I wasn't even thinking it. I was in the dream myself. But reality can't be thought away—what's real is rational, and what's rational is real. I can't describe to you my feelings when I heard those words. They were my release from my weary guardianship of the human race. I grasped the meaning of the rise and fall of kingdoms, the ebb and flow of history, the pettiness of my miserable anxiety about my life. Reality! I say it every night when I go to bed and every morning when I wake—and the reality for us, Michael, is that I'm the editor of the *Moscow Observer,* and you are a contributor. By all means continue to submit your articles. I will give them serious consideration.

MICHAEL   My God, I'm surrounded by egoists! Hegel lived so that Belinsky could sleep at night!?—so that this scribbling kopeck-counter can squeak 'Reality!' at me when my spirit is in chains and the whole world conspires against me with agriculture and . . . oh, God, I have to get to Berlin! That's the sole meaning of my life! Who will be my saviour? Is there nobody who sees that the future of philosophy in Russia hangs on lending me a few miserable roubles? Then you'll see! I'll show you all . . . !

Michael blunders out of the room and is heard stumbling and shouting his way down the stairs.

JUNE 1840

In atrocious weather Michael stands by the guardrail of a tender—a riverboat—with rain sluicing down on him from a black sky. On the shore, Herzen watches him. Michael has to shout against the storm.

MICHAEL   Goodbye! Goodbye, Herzen! Thank you! Goodbye, Russia! Goodbye.

JULY 1840

A street (St Petersburg).

Belinsky, hurrying away, crosses the path of Herzen, who carries a magazine journal.

HERZEN   Are you Belinsky?

BELINSKY   Yes.

HERZEN   I am Herzen. Our friend Bakunin has perhaps spoken of me.

BELINSKY (*flustered*)   Has he? Oh, yes, I see . . .

HERZEN   St Petersburg is a lonely city for us Moscovites . . . Still, with *National Notes* . . . (*He indicates his journal.*) you no longer have the cares of editorship. I'm sorry about the *Moscow Observer*, but to be honest, it made mental confusion uninteresting.

BELINSKY   Did you like any of it?

HERZEN   I liked the colour.

BELINSKY   That was Bakunin's idea. He's on his way to Germany now, I don't know how he managed it.

HERZEN   I saw him off on the tender to Kronstadt.

BELINSKY   That would be it. How much did you lend him?

HERZEN   A thousand.

BELINSKY (*laughs*)   When I have to borrow a hundred, the humiliation makes me ill. For Michael a new friend is the means of recuperation.

HERZEN   I met Bakunin at a charity ball where the guests were drinking toasts to the Hegelian categories, 'to Essence,' 'to Idea' . . . Six years ago when I went into exile, Hegel was hardly mentioned. Now you can't buy a bootlace without the shop-clerk asking your opinion of existence-in-itself. It was a fancy-dress ball. Until I'd seen a six-foot ginger cat raise its glass to Absolute Subjectivity, the full meaning of exile hadn't come home to me.

BELINSKY   Have you read my article?

HERZEN   And then there were your articles . . . To rail against the march of history was pointless and self-important, to deplore the unfortunate details was pedantic, and for art to concern itself was ridiculous . . . Evidently, Hegel was a philosopher I should study carefully. And what did I find? You've got Hegel's Dialectical Spirit of History upside down and so has he. People don't storm the Bastille because history proceeds by zigzags. History zigzags because when people have had enough, they storm the Bastille. When you turn him right way up, Hegel is the algebra of revolution. The Dialectical Spirit of History would be an extravagant redundancy even if one could imagine what sort of animal it was supposed to be . . . a gigantic ginger cat, for example.

Belinsky! . . . Belinsky! We're not the plaything of an imaginative cosmic force, but of a Romanov with no imagination whatsoever, a mediocrity. He's the sort of person you see behind a post office counter who points to the clock at one minute past five and won't sell you a stamp . . . and he's got the whole country quaking like a schoolroom under a sadistic pedagogue. Nowhere does authority feel freer, nothing restrains it, not shame before our neighbours nor the judgement of history. In the vilest autocracies in the worst of times, Spinoza wasn't flogged. Heine wasn't sent to the mines for a poem, no one came for Rousseau in the night for singing revolutionary songs at a drunken party. In the taxonomy of despotism, Russia is a genus to itself. The English flog their sailors and soldiers, too, but here we have floggings in the Institute of Engineers! Oh yes, I've read your articles. You've committed intellectual suicide.

BELINSKY Well, you have the moral right. Exile is your badge of honour—(*passionately*)—but I also suffer for what I think and write. For me, suffering and thinking are the same thing!

Herzen is chastened.

HERZEN In exile I lived the life of a minor official. My duties included countersigning the police reports on my supervision—I see why you insist that Gogol is a realist. I also fell in love, by letter post, and got married after a midnight elopement as romantic as anything in George Sand, and now our firstborn is a year old. I never had a better year in my life than my last year of exile. You have nothing to learn from me about suffering. But about the *Cat* . . . the Cat has no plan, no favourites or resentments, no memory, no mind, no rhyme or reason. It kills without purpose, and spares without purpose, too. So, when it catches your eye, what happens next is not up to the Cat, it's up to you. (*He nods farewell.*)

BELINSKY   I saw you once before. It was in the Zoo Gardens, you were with Stankevich . . . just before you were arrested.

HERZEN   That was the last time I saw Stankevich. We parted almost on a quarrel. That's a lesson to us. Forgive me if I spoke harshly about your . . .

BELINSKY   He's not dead, is he?

Pause. Belinsky cries out.

HERZEN   I'm sorry . . . yes . . . Granovsky's had a letter from . . . Berlin. Stankevich died in Italy a month ago.

Belinsky looks up at the sky and shakes his fists at it.

BELINSKY   Who is this Moloch that eats his children?

HERZEN   (*Pause.*)   It's the Ginger Cat. (*Herzen leaves.*)

A GINGER CAT, *smoking a cigar and holding a glass of champagne, watches Belinsky from a little distance. There is music.*

SPRING 1843

The stage fills with dancers and party guests passing through. 'Fancy dress' is de rigueur but in the main lightly honoured (a Shepherdess, a Spanish Lady, a Byron, a Cossack) rather than concealing identity, as in the case of the Ginger Cat, who really is a huge, upright disreputable cat . . . who soon moves out of view along with the throng, without Belinsky having noticed him.

Tatiana, Alexandra and Natalie are in an agitated, anxious huddle over a letter of several pages. Natalie reads and passes pages to Alexandra, who reads and gives them to Tatiana, who has already read the letter.

Varenka is dancing with Dyakov. Varvara enters, encountering Turgenev as a masked Harlequin. She cuts him, intent on intercepting Varenka. Turgenev leaves.

VARVARA (*to Varenka*)   Alexandra's dancing too many dances.

VARENKA   But she's dancing with her husband.

VARVARA   You don't know everything, you know.

VARENKA   You mean—? (*pleased*) Oh . . . !

Varenka abandons Dyakov, whom Varvara belatedly acknowledges.

VARVARA (*to Varenka*)   You don't know, you don't know!

Varenka hurries away. Dyakov offers his arm to Varvara.

VARVARA (*cont.*) (*to Dyakov*)   Well, I said all would be well, didn't I?—Varenka's back and you're together.

DYAKOV   I'm the happiest man in the world.

They leave together.

Chaadaev enters with Belinsky.

CHAADAEV   What is your costume, by the way?

BELINSKY   Sackcloth and ashes.

CHAADAEV   There's no shame in changing your opinion.

BELINSKY   Yes, I'm good at that, it's one of my best things. How is it that everybody but me knows what he thinks and sticks to it! I was wrestling with my angel while he whispered in my ear, 'Belinsky, Belinsky, the life and death of a single child weighs more than your whole construction of historical necessity.' I couldn't keep it up. I was broken by it.

CHAADAEV   But I meant changing your mind about Pushkin. You told me when he was still alive that it was over with him.

BEINSKY   I didn't know what he was going to give us from
the grave. But his time was up just the same. It's the age of
Pushkin which is over: that's why we all remember where
we were when we heard he was dead. I always believed that
the artist expresses his age by singing with no more purpose
than a bird. But now we need a new kind of song, a
different singer. Pushkin's Tatiana loves Onegin but stays
faithful to the dullard she married, a heroine to her creator.
Put her into George Sand and she'd be a joke, a dullard
herself, faithful to a moribund society—this from a man
who was once exiled for his poetry, and said if he hadn't
been in exile he would have joined the Decembrists! Well,
the man and the artist can no longer pass each other in the
doorway taking turns to be at home: there's only one
person under the roof, he can't be separated from himself,
and must be judged all together . . .

CHAADAEV   If I could bring Pushkin back to life by reducing
George Sand to a fine powder and sprinkling it on his grave,
I'd leave for Paris tonight with a coffee grinder in my luggage.

BELINSKY   Oh God, you're right, you're right!

In his fervour he embraces Chaadaev, unsteadying him.

CHAADAEV   Your changes of opinion are gaining speed, I
think I must go home before I fall over . . . and there's
another Tatiana waiting her turn . . .

Chaadaev bows to Tatiana as he leaves and she enters.

TATIANA   Vissarion . . . we thought Moscow had lost you forever.

BELINSKY   No, I . . . I'm just back to . . . To tell you the
truth, I'm getting married . . . No one you know. A young
woman.

TATIANA   But you're in love!

BELINSKY I wouldn't go so far as to say that.

TATIANA Then you must be lonely in St Petersburg.

BELINSKY I heard you'd been ill.

TATIANA Ill? . . . Yes . . . He's over there, on the balcony, can you see him? The Harlequin. He knew Michael in Berlin. He wants to be a poet.

BELINSKY Too tall, I'm afraid. Have you heard from Michael? He's discovered revolution!

TATIANA We never used to care about politics.

BELINSKY He doesn't care about them now. Revolution is his new philosophy of self-fulfilment.

TATIANA Will you wait for me?

Tatiana goes to Turgenev. Belinsky waits.

TATIANA (*cont.*) I only want to ask you something.

TURGENEV I am very glad to see you. Are you all right now?

TATIANA Yes. My letters must have been . . . tiresome.

TURGENEV You will always be . . .

TATIANA Your sister, your muse, yes . . . Well, it was just a fevered imagination. But even now it's a joy to remember. I lived with my whole heart and soul. Everything around me was transfigured. I will never be so happy, there's no philosophy which prepared me for it, so tell anybody you like that I loved you and laid my unasked-for love at your feet.

TURGENEV What did you . . . ?

TATIANA It's Michael. He's going to go to prison unless someone helps, and I don't know where else to . . .

TURGENEV How much?

TATIANA Four thousand roubles. I know you have already . . .

TURGENEV I can't pay it all.

TATIANA What should I write to him?

TURGENEV Half.

TATIANA Thank you.

TURGENEV (*shrugs*) Simplicity is always welcome. More and more. (*Pause.*) There's a miller's wife . . . I met her when I was out shooting in the country outside Petersburg . . . She would never accept anything from me. But one day she said to me, 'You ought to give me a present.' 'What would you like?' I said. 'Bring me some scented soap from St Petersburg,' she replied. So, next time, I did. She ran off with it, and came back presently all pink in the face, and, with her lightly scented hands stretched out to me, she said, 'Kiss my hands as you kiss the hands of your fine Petersburg ladies . . .' I knelt before her . . . I don't think I've experienced a lovelier moment in the whole of my life.

Tatiana runs away in tears. Turgenev sees Belinsky waiting and approaches him.

TURGENEV (*cont.*) Are you Belinsky? Forgive me . . . I would be honoured if you would accept . . .

Turgenev takes a small book from his pocket and presents it with a small bow. Belinsky takes it and looks at it.

BELINSKY You are a poet?

TURGENEV That's for you to say. As you see, I am perhaps unnecessarily shy about meeting my readers in my true identity . . .

BELINSKY But . . . surely you don't always go about in . . . ?

TURGENEV I mean on the title page.

BELINSKY Of course. (*He opens the book.*) 'Parasha' . . . (*He turns to the first lines.*) 'I do not like ecstatic young women . . . I dislike their pale round faces . . .'

TURGENEV It's the first thing in my own voice. (*He bows.*) Ivan Turgenev. You are our only critic.

Turgenev leaves.

The Ginger Cat, smoking a cigar, is left behind by a group of guests who cross the stage. Belinsky and the Ginger Cat look at each other for a long moment.

BELINSKY Belinsky.

The Ginger Cat takes the cigar from his mouth.

GINGER CAT Of course.

They continue to look at each other.

AUTUMN 1844

Premukhino, before sunset.

Semyon and Servants place chairs to face the sunset. Alexander, aged seventy-six, enters from the house.

ALEXANDER Another sunset, another season nearer God.

Varvara appears and calls from the house.

VARVARA What are you doing? You'll catch your death!

ALEXANDER We're going to see the sun go down. Vasilly says it's tomorrow the weather's due to turn.

VARVARA   Come inside—I never heard such nonsense.

ALEXANDER   What's nonsense about it?

Semyon moves a chair out of Alexander's path just in time.

ALEXANDER (*cont.*)   Who's there? Semyon?

SEMYON   Yes, sir.

ALEXANDER   Good man.

He puts out his hand. Semyon kisses it.

ALEXANDER (*cont.*)   No, you fool, where is it?

Semyon guides Alexander into one of the chairs.

VARVARA   I'll tell you what's nonsense about it. First, there's no sun, and second, if there were any sun, you couldn't see it. And to top it off, Vasilly's been dead for years.

ALEXANDER   He stocked up when he knew the end was near. (*Pause.*) Has he? Of course. Who's our forester now?

VARVARA   You sold the forest.

ALEXANDER   Sit by me.

Varvara returns to the house.

ALEXANDER (*cont.*)   'The moon is up and yet it is not night . . .' Who's there?

SEMYON   May I beg your honour the favour to ask you, sir . . . There's talk there's a levy ordered from the Army, sir. No one wants to go for a soldier, your honour—our young lads are in a terror of it, and the mothers are worse . . . if it's true, sir . . . ?

ALEXANDER (*angrily*)   Too proud to serve their country, is it? If I hear any more I'll volunteer the lot of them, levy or no levy!—If they stole less and worked more, I could afford the redemption ticket when the levy comes round, and let my neighbours send their souls to go soldiering instead.

Semyon kneels and hugs Alexander's legs.

SEMYON Forgiveness, your honour! Have pity!

Tatiana comes from the house with a rug.

TATIANA What now? Mother says put this round you. (*Tatiana puts the rug round him.*)

ALEXANDER Snooping at my letters! (*to Semyon*) That's enough.

TATIANA You know he can't read. What is it, Semyon . . . ?

Semyon leaves, bowing his way backwards.

ALEXANDER It was the eagle. Wasn't it?—the eagle embossed on the envelope, and none of your wood-pulp paper—fine linen, heavy as cream. They're like children, the bogeyman is everywhere come to get them. Go on with you, old friend . . . and tell those gossips it wasn't the levy, the Emperor has worse to communicate to their innocent master.

TATIANA Semyon's gone, Father. I'll tell him. (*Tatiana gets up, but her attention is caught.*) Oh—look! The cloud's lifting . . .

Sunshine—weak and nearly red.

TATIANA (*cont.*) Just in time!

ALEXANDER I can see it.

TATIANA What was the letter?

ALEXANDER Like the bonfire.

TATIANA Was it about Michael?

ALEXANDER Michael isn't coming home again. Premukhino knows it, too. The spirit has left it. You grew up in Paradise, all of you children, in harmony that was the wonder of all who came here. Then, in the time of Liubov's betrothal to that cavalry officer—what was his name? . . . and what was the point in the end? Michael . . . (*Pause.*) Or a new spirit, which is worse . . . (*Pause.*) I got the priest to read it to me, so to be ready when I tell your mother. Michael was invited to the Russian Legation in Berne to receive an official summons to return home . . . for getting mixed up with some socialist rabble-rouser they had there in Switzerland. Fancy! Among all those pretty cows and mountains and cheese. Michael's in Paris now, it seems. Criminal proceedings were started against him in St Petersburg. No one told me. By imperial decree, former Ensign Michael Bakunin has been condemned to loss of his noble rank and to banishment to Siberia for an indefinite period, with hard labour . . . and his property is declared confiscated to the State. What can they mean by that?

Tatiana takes his hand and after a moment wipes her eyes with it.

ALEXANDER (*cont.*) Sun's gone. Has it?

Tatiana nods.

ALEXANDER (*cont.*) I saw it go down.

TATIANA Yes.

ALEXANDER Has it set?

TATIANA Yes. I said yes.

Fade to black.